For Rachel and Eli who like to eat potatoes

For an explanatory leaflet about Homœopathy contact:
The Society of Homœopaths, 2 Artizan Road, Northampton NN1 4HU.
Telephone 01604 21400

CONTENTS

LIST OF ILLUSTRATIONS

1 INTRODUCTION

This book began as a lecture given at the Irish Homœopathic Conference on 1 July 1995 at University College Galway. My talk aroused much interest and emotion. 1995 was the chosen year for the 150th anniversary commemoration of the potato famine in Ireland. Homœopaths were as much involved in the coming to terms with the past as the rest of the population. I decided to respond and develop my ideas and sources into a book.

At the conclusion of the first conference in Galway in 1994 I surprised the audience with the presentation to the Irish Society of Homœopaths of a facsimile copy of the first English language edition of the *Organon*. This was translated from the 4th German edition and was published in Dublin in 1833.[1] I called Dr Jacques Baur in Lyon, France, and persuaded him to make me a copy.[2] This was presented to the Irish Society of Homœopaths as a gift from the UK Society of Homœopaths. Some little time later a book dealer called me with the offer of an original. I had to act quickly so I called Nuala Eising, Principal of the Burren School of Homœopathy and a copy of this old and venerable book is now back in Ireland. I know nothing of its origins and how it came to be published in Dublin except that Dublin was one of the cultural capitals of Europe at that

---

[1] Samuel Hahnemann, *The homœopathic medical doctrine or organon of the healing art*, translated by Charles H Devrient from the 4th German edition of 1829, with notes by Samuel Stratten; Dublin, W F Wakeman, 1833
[2] Jacques Baur, *Un livre sans frontières; histoire et métamorphose de l'Organon de Hahnemann*, Lyon, Éditions Boiron, 1991

time. With no conscious knowledge of what was to come I agreed to speak about the history of homœopathy in Ireland at the 1995 conference.

And what did come was an unsolicited letter from a descendant of the most distinguished homœopath ever to come from Ireland whose work is discussed in this book. He enclosed some family papers and wondered if they might be of interest! We were honoured by the presence of one of his descendants at the conference, Dr Emilia Kidd. I am forever indebted to Mr C M Kidd.

I should like to thank the participants of the conference for their positive response to my talk which spurred me on to prepare this for publication. I should like to thank Michael Thompson for his insights into the remedy *Solanum tuberosum aegrotans*, and his help in producing the repertory summary analysis. I should like to thank John Churchill for all his advice about book publishing over the years. Vivienne Rawnsley has created a great design. Steve at Candor is working wonders with the plans for printing and binding. Most of all I should like to thank Rachel for her forbearance and support while I was preparing the lecture, and for her help in producing the book which included voluntarily typing all the original sources, and photographing a heap of rotting potatoes.

So now to homœopathy. I am not going to give you a timetabled history of homœopathy in Ireland. I am not even going to tell you that only a few miles from Galway at Ennis, a Dr Greene was the first to use *Crataegus*[3]. Rather I am going to tell you some *craic*, some stories; not all of them are about Ireland directly but you will see how the stories relate to each other.

Francis Treuherz MA MCH RSHom FSHom
London, August 1995

---

[3] John Henry Clarke, *Dictionary of homœopathic materia medica*; London, Homœopathic Publishing Co, 3 volumes, 1900 & 1925

2   BENOÎT MURE, ADVENTURES IN HOMŒOPATHY

INTRODUCTION
By FRANCIS TREUHERZ

A question

In what circumstances might you dream of eating human flesh?

Perhaps in a condition of famine and starvation? Because of the potato blight. Many of you will know that Ireland suffered a unique tragedy 150 years ago. I can liken it to the holocaust suffered by my people, the Jews; or the displacement of indigenous Americans. The exciting cause was a fungal infestation of the potato.

Ireland had been one of the most densely populated countries in Europe despite having very little industry and despite the general poverty and previous more localised famines. Land was apportioned into small lots by rapacious landlords so that where arable crops were grown they were sold to pay the rent and the produce was exported. The mass of the people lived in squalor and ate potatoes and buttermilk. In 1845 the potato crop failed. In 1846 and 1847 it failed again more drastically. As a result hundreds of thousands of people died from destitution and starvation. Even more died from typhus, relapsing or continuing fever and bacillary dysentery. Yet more emigrated and perhaps 20% of these died en route or on arrival. The enormity of the tragedy cannot be underestimated. The population shrank by some 2.5 million people.

I wept when I read the detailed history by Cecil Woodham Smith which I commend to those of you who have not come across this story before.[1] I felt humble as a guest among the homœopaths of Ireland, whose ancestors lived through those years. Some readers will have a miasmatic memory of this catastrophe. Others will know little of it.

Benoît Mure,

It was only in 1849 that an adventurous homœopath named Benoît Mure (1809-1858, only 49 years), carried out a proving on the diseased potato, *Solanum tuberosum aegrotans.*[2] It was another 5 years before Hempel's translation was published. It will be interesting to digress for a moment to mention Mure's achievements. Mure came from Lyon in France and were it not for linguistic barriers would be better known in our community.[3] He had a brilliant and inventive mind, created succussion and trituration machinery, and an indecipherable so called *Logarithm Repertory.*[4]

He studied with Des Guidi, the father of French homœopathy, and with Hahnemann himself. He travelled widely, especially in Malta, Sicily, Egypt and what concerns us here, South America, where he organised provings of some 38 substances and laid the foundations for the growth of homœopathy in that continent.

I mention something of his work so that you can appreciate the context for his idea of the purposes of proving *Solanum tuberosum aegrotans*. Mure wrote:-

"Human pathology is not the only field of the homœopathist. He should take an interest in every species of suffering, and endeavour to restore the harmony of the organic kingdom, wherever it has been

---

[1] Cecil Woodham Smith, *The great hunger; Ireland 1845-1849*, London, Hamish Hamilton 1962, Penguin, 1991

[2] Benoît Mure, *Materia medica or provings of the principal animal and vegetable poisons of the Brazilian Empire and their application in the treatment of disease*, Translated by Charles J Hempel, New York, William Radde; London, James Epps; & Manchester, Henry Turner, 1854

[3] Roseline Brillat, *Benoît Mure, missionaire de l'homéopathie, 1809-1858*, Lyon, Éditions Boiron, 1988

[4] Benoît Mure & Sophie Liet, *L'Homéopathie pure,* Paris, J B Ballière et fils, 1883

disturbed by some accidental cause. The healing art is one; there is no such thing as one healing art for man and another for the animal, though it is on man that we should prove our drugs because he is the complex of the various kingdoms of nature.

The question now occurs, how is the potato-rot to be treated? It is evident that the great point is to *prevent* the disease, and for this purpose, we must endeavour to remove the cause."

He went on to discuss creating a proving on the potato itself but rejected this idea.

The veterinary homœopathist does very well in selecting his remedy by the human pathogenesis. Why should not the same mode be applicable to vegetables?

Following an analysis of his provings he suggests that we may inoculate the potato as we put it in the ground either with the most similar remedies namely *Bryonia* or *Arsenicum*, or his new nosode, as a way of preventing the rot!

Mure's own *Materia Medica*, and Clarke's *Dictionary*[5] are the chief sources which you can study for yourselves later in this book. I am aware that homœopaths in Ireland have begun to study and use this remedy. It is related as a vegetable nosode to *Secale*, (ergot of rye) and *Ustilago maidis*, (corn smut). I have found almost no references in our literature save for a case by the erudite Erastus Case in an old journal.[6] He gave a 1M potency to a woman of 40 with early menses on the gounds of the odour of the menses, of decayed fish.

I have not been able to discover whether there was any connection in the 19th century, between the proving described here, and the subsequent use of the remedy in Ireland.

---

[5] John Henry Clarke, *Dictionary of homœopathic materia medica,* London, Homœopathic Publishing Co, 3 volumes, 1900 & 1925
[6] Erastus Case, Bureau of materia medica, *Transactions of International Hahnamannian Association,* 1915 page 175.

The Proving

SOLANUM TUBEROSUM ÆGROTANS
Sol-t-æ. Diseased Potato
By Benoît Mure[7]

A description of the potato in a work destined for European pharmaceutists and physicians, would be entirely useless; so well and so universally known is this plant in Europe. However since our work will get into the hands of persons who are less familiar with the productions of the European continent, we deem it advisable to subjoin a short description of this plant. The potato is a native of Chile; it is an herbaceous plant, with a branchy stem about one or two feet high. Its leaves are pinnatifid, with leaflets that are oval, entire, slightly hairy on their lower surface and almost opposite. Smaller folioles sometimes arise between the larger ones. The flowers constitute corymbs either erect or inclined; calice in five parts; corol of a white violet with five equal divisions; five stamens attached to the basis of the corol; one style and stigma, fleshy berry with two chambers. The roots develop tubercles of different sizes and called potatoes. The potato-rot first reveals itself by brown spots irregularly distributed through the interior of the tubercles; gradually these spots are transformed into white points of a cottony appearance which may be compared to the cryptogamia termed byssus, and found on damp wood. From this point a general process of decomposition sets in, and the potato exhales an insupportable nauseous odour. In our provings we have made use of a potato in an entire state of decomposition, without however, being completely rotten; there were brown portions intermingled with those byssus-shaped parts described above.

HOMŒOPATHIC TREATMENT OF POTATO ROT
Human pathology is not the only field of the homœopathist. He should take an interest in every species of suffering, and endeavour to restore the harmony of the organic kingdom wherever it has been disturbed by some accidental cause. Homœopathy is a vast unitary science. The healing art is one; there is no such thing as one healing art for man and another for the

---

[7] Benoît Mure 1854 op.cit.

animal, though it is on man that we should prove our drugs because he is the complex of the various kingdoms of nature.

The question now occurs, how is the potato-rot to be treated? It is evident that the great point is to *prevent* the disease, and, for this purpose, we must endeavour to remove the cause. *Principiis obsta*, has ever been the fundamental rule of medical treatment.

In order to attain this end we have deemed it necessary first to ascertain the effects which the diseased potato would produce in a healthy person and afterwards to find out what drugs produce similar effects. We might have instituted our provings on the potato itself, and, among a number of drugs, might have discovered the one that would produce a disease similar to the rot. But this mode of investigation would have been too long and uncertain, whereas the proving on the human body is simple and direct, and is, we think, the true mode which Providence has designed we should pursue even in regard to the potato-rot.

It is true, man cannot be assimilated to the myriads of organised beings that surround us; man constitutes the highest link in the chain of beings; he is the complex of the animal life on our globe, and the most perfect type to which all inferior existences can be referred; he is a microcosm containing all the wonders of the universe; he is the responsible administrator of this earth. Man alone is able to produce a true pathogenesis by revealing the most evanescent as well as the most characteristic and most permanent symptoms, or lesions of sensation. On plants and animals we can only perceive disordered functions, disorganisations of tissues, or acute pains as manifested by gestures or cries; but the truly dynamic action can only be properly perceived and described by man.

The veterinary homœopathist does very well in selecting his remedy by the human pathogenesis. Why should not the same mode be applicable to vegetables? We have invited our fellow-beings to try it; we have not only invited them to teach, and to cure, and to make themselves sick, in order to discover the true means of healing; but we have encouraged them to suffer themselves to be persecuted, and even imprisoned, as a reward for their labours of love, we have said to them; whilst the world is hesitating whether

7

it should accept or reject the blessing offered by Hahnemann, let us lose no time; there are other regions where the evil is still triumphant, and where truth is not even known by name; let us expel error from its last hiding places. And we have never failed in meeting corresponding souls that would hear us and follow us. And thus it is that homœopathy, this physical reflex of the Christian redemption combats evil by itself, pursuing it from region to region until it shall have been exterminated from the world.

Now let us describe the practical part of our proving.

From the first, frontal headaches, with pressure above the orbits, have been observed with much regularity not only by the three provers whose symptoms are published, but also by other provers who continued the proving only for a few days.

Until the 20th day, these headaches were often accompanied by fever, with chill, heat, sweat, shudderings followed by sore throat, cough and greenish mucous expectoration.

The palpitation of the heart which occurs during the whole period of the proving, and with particular violence at the end of the third proving, appears to be represented in the case of the second prover by violent muscular pulsations occurring in the same chronological order. The hard, large sized, fragmentary stools, and their painful expulsion which sometimes caused a falling of the rectum; the frequent emission of flatulence preceded or accompanied by colic, with sensitiveness of the abdominal integuments in the case of the first prover, are very constant symptoms of this drug; they were observed from the first and increased until the last days of the proving.

We will likewise point to the general or partial weakness, which, in the case of the third prover, were followed by violent pains in the loins.

The white coating of the tongue which was observed on the first day, gradually limited itself to a yellow line along the middle. Among the less general symptoms which were observed during the whole time of the proving, we may note the want of appetite, the bitter taste of food, the cutaneous eruptions, the swelling of the mucous membrane of the palate, the thick urine, and lastly the pain in the groin or the right ileo-femoral articulation.

In the emotive sphere the drug induced a great irritability. The dreams about a change of form occurred very generally to the three provers. The second prover had the same dream on two successive nights.

After careful comparison of the symptoms of the *Solanum tubersosum ægrotans* with those of the other known remedies of our Materia Medica, we have found them to agree with the symptoms of the following drugs which we enumerate in the order of their importance.

1. *Bryonia*
2. *Arsenicum*
3. *Plumbum*
4. *Nux vomica*
5. *Sepia*
6. *Strontiana*
7. *Viola tricolor*
8. *Squilla*
9. *Pulsatilla*
10. *Graphites*
11. *Alumina*
12. *Mercurius*
13. *Natrum muriaticum*
14 *Ignatia*
15. *Calcarea.*

We have no doubt that *Bryonia* and *Arsenicum* will prevent the rot; but to be frank, we believe that, in this case at least, the isopathic method of treatment will prove more successful than the homœopathic. It is well known that the mode of preparing our drugs for medicinal purposes, modifies their action a good deal. This result is principally obtained by rubbing them down with sugar of milk, which is not an inert substance as Hahnemann believed, but is on the contrary endowed with the most useful powers of action. The sugar of milk effects a preliminary digestion of the drug, and by imparting to it vital qualities, fits it for medicinal purposes. Do we not know that certain animal products are preferable to corresponding mineral substances? Is not the *Calcarea* prepared from the oyster-shell preferable to the chemically prepared carbonates and phosphates of lime? Are not the poisons of serpents destined to occupy the first rank among the polychrests?

To return to our subject, the medicinal preparation obtained from the diseased potato is not the original poison as used by nature, but the poison modified in consequence of its having been previously engrafted on a living tubercle.

Our mode of inoculating either the isopathic or homœopathic preparation is as follows. Before putting the potato in the ground we perforate it with a big needle, and into this hole we insert a single globule of the third attenuation.

This operation is simple and easy. It can be applied on a large scale, and we think that by its means the potato will be preserved for a long time yet to the European continent.

First prover: *Van-Dyck*, 26 years old, of a sanguine nervous temperament and a robust constitution.

First day. Painful stitch in the right side, a few moments after taking the drug. Acidity and eructations, at 9 in the evening.

Second day. On waking, weight above the eyes and in the forehead, as the morning after being intoxicated. Shuddering and sensation of cold internally at noon. Scanty and difficult stool, in the shape of small hard balls, in the evening.

Third day. He dreams he is to dress and draw the body of a drowned man; this body bounded up every moment and fell back either on his clothes or on his drawing board. The mucous membrane of the palate seems to detach itself here and there. Cross; he blames everything and cannot bear that anything near him should be disturbed.

Fourth day. Difficult stool in small red balls.

Fifth day. Stool as above.

Sixth day. Horrid colic, as if the bowels were violently twisted; 15 minutes after, hard and copious stool, followed by two almost liquid stools (at night).

Seventh day. Copious and liquid diarrhœa, of a greenish yellow, in the morning. Prickling around the eyelids; on their internal surface they are red and congested. Tongue coated white. White sordes on the teeth. (Profuse lachrymation). Little appetite. Pulse rather agitated.

Eighth day. The median line of the abdomen from the sternum to the hypogastrium is painful to the touch. Thirst. Little appetite. Sensation of warmth about the head at 4 in the evening.

Ninth day. Dreams about magic, men being transformed into speaking animals, changes at night, etc. Heat in the canal of the urethra, after urinating. The urine deposits a yellowish sediment. Small pimples on the back, causing a violent itching. Sneezing in going upstairs.

Tenth day. Heaviness on the eyes. Slight beating in the temples. Mounting of heat to the head from time to time.

Eleventh day. Pricking around the eyelids on waking. Itching of the back. Sweat on doing the least work. Heaviness of the head.

Twelfth day. Heaviness in the head which is at times most violent, especially when raising the head again after stooping. Smarting and prickling in the eyes. No stool for five days past.

Thirteenth day. Heaviness of the head worse in the morning than the evening. Ordinary stool. Difficult digestion. Sneezing after going upstairs. Likes to loiter about.

Fourteenth day. Heaviness of the head. Ordinary stool. He would like to go to bed, but is too lazy at ten in the evening. Pains in the thighs, above the kneepan.

Fifteenth day. (Lachrymation on waking). Slight heaviness of the head. Greenish yellow coating on the tongue along the middle. White slime on the teeth. Headache at noon. Lancinations in the region of the heart. Chilliness with chattering of the teeth. Smarting at the eyes, in the evening. Not much appetite. Sneezing. Lips cracked, bleeding and almost raw.

Sixteenth day. Smarting at the eyelids. Tongue slightly coated white. White mucous on the teeth. Dreams about his daily business. Flatulence and eructations. Agitated pulse. Sneezing at 4 in the afternoon. Smarting and prickling at the eyes.

Seventeenth day. Colic followed by two stools at 4 in the morning. The right umbilical region is painful to contact.

Eighteenth day. Colic. Not much appetite. Sneezing at 5 in the evening.

Nineteenth day. Prickling in the throat, inducing cough. Dry cough

Twenty-third day. Heaviness of the head on waking.

Twenty-fourth day. Headache aggravated by the smell of alcohol and disappearing at 3 in the evening.

Twenty-fifth day. Colic on waking. Frequent emission of flatulence. Pains between the shoulders (at 10 in the evening).

Twenty-sixth day. He dreams that his hands are cut in pieces. Tickling in the throat causing a cough.

Second Prover: *Charles Dieudonné Jolly*, 24 years old, nervous-sanguine temperament, robust constitution.

First day. Pressure at the root of the nose. Dreams about religious things.

Second day. Heaviness of the head, in the morning. The head and especially the forehead, feel dull as during a catarrh, all the afternoon. Colic after eating. Sexual dream, followed by a dream about women that are changed to animals.

Third day. Frequent emission of flatulence, in the morning. Tongue slightly coated white, in the morning. Colic and twisting in the stomach after eating. Salt taste in the throat. Pressure in the forehead and above the orbits.

Fifth day. Slight yellowish-white coating on the tongue, in the morning. Heat in the face, at half past four in the afternoon. Pain as if sprained at the right, coxo-femoral articulation, posteriorly. Flow of ideas at 5. Beating at the middle portion of the triceps brachialis, at 8.

Seventh day. Wakes very early since the third day. Itching at the ball of the thumb at 9 in the evening.

Eighth day. Wakes very early. Thin yellowish coating on the tongue in the morning. Prickling in the lumbar muscles at 6 in the afternoon.

Ninth day. Stitch in the left ring finger at 7 in the morning. Stitch and sharp pinching in the right groin, near the inguinal ring; this pain was felt shortly after an ordinary stool, while raising one leg as if one would mount three steps at once, at 11 in the morning. Beating in the left thigh at 4 in the afternoon, while sitting. Drowsy at half past 7, waking very early.

Tenth day. Beating under the right shoulder, at 9 in the evening. Drowsy at 8 o'clock in the evening

Eleventh day. Weight in the left testicle, the whole day, also in the evening while sitting.

Twelfth day. Violent pulsations at the lowest part of the vastus internus muscle in a demi-circle, for an hour and a half in the morning.

Thirteenth day. Beating in the lumbar muscles at 4 in the afternoon.

Fourteenth day. Headache. Repeated sneezing at half past 8 in the evening.

Fifteenth day. Sense of weariness in the muscles of the right thigh, after walking. Involuntary crowding of heterogenous ideas on one's mind while listening to a discourse or attending to some work; frequently during the proving.

Sixteenth day. Tongue coated white in the morning. Contraction and beating at the left superior eyelid, at 7 in the evening. Slight colic and copious flatulence all night.

Seventeenth day. Restless sleep. Flatulence in the evening. Hard and scanty stool.

Eighteenth day. He dreams that he will fall from a tower. Violent beating of the heart in raising himself. Pricking in the right side of the tongue, from noon until 3. Roughness in the throat, with thirst, in the evening. Cough and yellowish mucus expectoration at night.

Nineteenth day. He dreams that he is in danger of falling from the roof of a house. Swelling of the mucous membrane of the internal alveolar margin of the two incisores and the left canine tooth. Violent frontal headache and coryza all day. Pain as if sprained at the right scapulo-humeral articulation, after having rested on the elbow, in the evening, in bed. Restless night.

Twentieth day. Confused dreams. Agitated pulse in the morning. Coryza.

Twenty-first day. Confused dreams, Frontal headache. Coryza. Agitated pulse. Sweats all over, in the morning, in bed. Strong pulsations at the perineum, loins, and right ring-finger at half past 4. Violent frontal headache at 5 in the afternoon, while walking. Large, hard, fragmentary stool. Urinates all the time during stool.

Twenty-third day. Strong pulsations in the vertebral region in the morning while lying. Whizzing in the left ear at 5 in the evening. Disposed to remember past journeys; flow of ideas about theories, etc.

Twenty-fourth day. Aching pain in the right hypo-gastric region, towards the ring, after a long walk.

Twenty-fifth day. Reddish urine, with mucus floating in it.

Third Prover: *Mme Al. J***,* **26 years old, of sanguine temperament, good constitution**.

First day. Tearing in the chest and throat, immediately.

Second day. Sexual dream. Dull colic in the hypo-gastric region, at night.

Third day. Dream about witchcraft. Difficult digestion accompanied by twisting in the stomach, after breakfast and dinner. Hard and knotty stool; after stool, renewed urging with smarting at the anus. Falling of the rectum. Sense of contraction at the sphincter. After stool, the rectum alternately descends and returns again. The falling of the rectum is accompanied by shuddering all over, for ten minutes.

Fifth day. Palpitation of the heart, at 11 in the evening, while lying.

Sixth day. Palpitation of the heart, at 7 in the morning. Colic at the stomach after eating, at 6 in the evening.

Seventh day. Tearing in the throat, at 8 in the morning. Tongue coated white.

Eighth day. Restless sleep; she dreams that she is eating human flesh. The least thing puts her out of humour. Palpitations of the heart, at noon. Palpitations of the heart at 11 in the evening, at three different periods.

Ninth day. Thick tongue at 2 in the morning.

Eleventh day. Restless sleep. Cold sweat at night, while lying.

Twelfth day. Sense of spraining in the ileo-femoral articulation, causing a pain in the womb; while making a trifling exertion. Flatulence; sometimes is unable to expel them. Headache. Contraction of the sphincter ani. Lancinating pain at the forehead, until 9 in the evening. Twisting colic. Stool always hard and difficult. Heat at the anus after stool. Weeping of the right eye, for some minutes. Frequent urging to stool. Shuddering all over, every moment, at 9 in the evening. Eructations in the evening. Flatulence in the evening. Quarrelsome mood.

Thirteenth day. No sleep. Heat all over, with sweat. Agitated pulse. She dreams that she is floating in a river and cannot get out. Flushes of heat in the face, now and then, especially while eating. These flushes are followed by chilliness. (Is unable to close her hand). Irregular pulse, at times feeble, at others strong. Frontal headache with dullness and disposition to incline forwards. Lazy. Weary all over, she has to lie down, at noon. Little appetite. Pressure at the chest. Thirst. Shivering while drinking cold water, or washing her face with it. Headache ceasing for a while and then recommencing again. Lancinations with sensation as if the brain would fly to pieces in going up-stairs. Vivid redness on the right malar eminence. Small red pimples on the cheeks. shuddering now and then. Congestion of the sclerotica. Red face at three in the evening. Flush of heat all over at half past 3. Sensation, while stooping as if the brain would bound in the skull. Heat at the vertex, which spreads all over, at 4. Sensation in the left hypochondrium as if a spring were rolled out. Sense of fainting, she has to stand still. Acute pain in the right pectoralis major when drawing breath. Borborygmi. Twisting of the bowels, at half past 10. Colic and shuddering. Dry cough in the evening. Headache decreases in the evening. Flatulence. Red and hot face. The skin of the face peels slightly.

Fourteenth day. Heat at night, disturbing the sleep. Sense of weariness in the limbs upon waking. Dullness of the forehead. Tongue coated white. In the morning, taste of raw potatoes. Menstrual blood rose-coloured, at 9 in the morning. Borborygmi, in the morning. At the least movement she feels as if a hollow body were turning rapidly round in the chest with a rattling noise; she then fancies she will faint, at 8 in the morning. Frontal headache all day. Smarting and painful sensation at the fifth dorsal vertebra, when clothes rub against part. Little appetite. Stiffness of the posterior cervical muscles. Dark redness and warmth of the cheeks. Heat all over in cold and damp weather. The menstrual flow is interrupted. Repeated sneezing, followed by a slight cough, every evening at 5, from the tenth day. Smell of blood, as if nosebleed would take place, at 7 in the morning.

Fifteenth day. Restless sleep. Last evening's dinner does not sit well on her stomach, with acidity at night. Doughy mouth in the morning. Weariness all over, when rising, drawing pain in the right lower limb, posteriorly, from the gluteus maximus to the heel. The menstrual flow is interrupted. when bending the knee, pulling pain in the posterior and internal muscles of the thigh. Hypochondria. Sadness. Every thing is disagreeable to her, she would like to go far away. Small pimples on the lower part of the neck and on the right knee, they are very red at the base, with a white point in the centre; they disappear in an hour. Sense of weight in the nape of the neck, at half past 11. The head feels heavy, she can scarcely keep it erect. Pain as from weariness in the back and the posterior muscles of the thighs and arms. Dullness of the head. Pain as if bruised, hindering her movements in bed. Very hot hands. Slight nosebleed, at 11 in the morning. She walks with difficulty, she fears, she will lose her muscular powers. The pain is worse in the day-time and less in the evening. The menstrual flow is interrupted. The epidermis of the face peels off. Numerous small pimples on the face. Desire to stretch.

Sixteenth day. No sleep; disturbed sleep. Oppression, owing to the dinner of last evening not sitting well on her stomach, she has to rise at 3 in the morning. Eructations followed by rumbling in the stomach, ceasing after drinking a glass of water with sugar. Tongue coated white, with a yellow line along the middle. (She would like to break everything, on account of not being able to understand a certain phrase). Doughy mouth, in the night. Alternate heat and shuddering in the night. (Has the taste of potatoes in the mouth, all night, from last evening's dinner). Beating in the left temple. Stiffness in the posterior cervical muscles. The sacrum is painful when touched or during a walk. After eating, choking and difficulty of breathing, caused by dryness of the mouth. Very fine pimples and intolerable itching at the labia majora.

Seventeenth day. Restless sleep. Is roused at 4 in the morning by a stomach-ache with eructations, for an hour. Headache during a half-slumber. Heaviness at the vertex in the evening. Shuddering and burning, in the evening in bed. Palpitation of the heart, while lying down. Ringing in the ears as if she would faint. Acute, stitch-like pain in the left side, preventing her from turning about in bed. The hair in the axilla sticks together.

Eighteenth day. Heaviness at the vertex. Disturbed sleep. Pain at the stomach and redness of the face after breakfast.

Nineteenth day. Feels well all over. Prickings at the right internal surface of the sternum.

Twentieth day. Sore throat; she is unable to swallow her saliva, in the evening. Distressing pain in the lumbar region, she cannot keep herself erect.

Twenty-first day. She feels as if a piece of flesh had grown out in her throat. Lancinating pain in the left iliac region, less in the right. Good appetite. Is unable to walk erect. Complains a good deal about her pain in the loins.

Twenty-second day. She is waked by a violent, shrill cough which lasts five hours. The pains in the loins are worse when stooping. Acute pain as if the sacrum were out of place. The pain in her loins causes her to cry out; she walks bent forward at 11. The least movement causes her an acute pain in the sacro-lumbar articulation. Pain in the posterior part of the right thigh as if a penknife were thrust in. Pain in the left gluteus muscle, accompanied by nausea. Sensation as if something would become detached from the sacrum. She can neither remain standing nor sitting. Pressure as from an iron bar at the sacro-lumbar articulation, obliging her to lie down when she feels better. Formication at the sacrum.Cough as from obstruction of the pharynx.

Twenty-third day. Restless sleep. Acute lancinating pain above the right breast, for two hours, in the morning. Pain as if sprained all along the vertebral column, and extending down the posterior muscles of the lower limbs to the heels. The face is dark red. She walks inclined forwards. Heaviness in the stomach, her dinner does not sit well on her stomach, at 9 in the evening Walking is hindered by the pain in the lumbar vertebræ. Desire for coffee.

Twenty-fourth day. Her dinner hurts her all night. Palpitation of the heart, in the night, three different times. Colic with loud emission of flatulence. Incoherent dreams. The pain in the loins is less. Twisting pain through the uterus, at nine in the evening.

Twenty-fifth day. Itching, wakes her at four in the morning.

Dreams about a witch, actors changing to yellow and black, Sense of spraining in the right groin. Slight nosebleed, at six in the evening. Thick urine, with appearance of white mucus some time after standing.

Twenty-sixth day. Dreams about fire, then a comedy. The urine continues to show white flocks after standing.

Twenty-seventh day. Slight nosebleed after supper. Violent itching at the labia majora at two.

Twenty-ninth day. Hard, difficult and large stool.

Thirtieth day. Dreams about a revolution, about a city being destroyed by fire and the sword. Sour eructations exciting her cough. Smarting and itching at the vulva, at two in the afternoon.

Thirty-second day. Canine hunger at dinner. Acidity, bitterness and regurgitations after dinner. Hard and large stool. Difficult fragmentary stool. Painful stool, making the tears rush to her eyes; the sclerotica becomes red in consequence of the efforts she is obliged to make. Soapy, pale-yellow urine. Colic along the large gut, at nine in the evening.

Thirty-third day. Pulling at the stomach, at two in the morning. Mouth dry. Large, dry, hard, difficult stool. Stool breaking off after one half is expelled. Pain and smarting at the rectum, caused by the violent efforts required to expel the stool. Not disposed to work, at eight in the evening. Irresistible drowsiness. Turbid urine, of a dingy-yellow and covered with an oily pellicle. Dreams about persecutions. Stitches during sleep as though needles were stuck in the spinal marrow; this wakes her. Starting during sleep. Dry mouth with tearing sensation in the chest, at two in the morning She rises in the night, imagining that thieves are hidden behind the curtains, but she dares not look behind and begs somebody else to do it.

Thirty-fourth day. Restless sleep. Anxiety on waking. Cracked tongue in the morning. Violent palpitations and pulsations with sensation as though the heart were turning about very briskly. The flatulence presses on the uterus. Hard, dry, large stool, expelled with difficulty, and causing the tears to rush to her eyes. Regurgitations and eructations at three. Noisy flatulence at nine in the evening.

Thirty-fifth day. Light sleep. Hoarseness on waking. White-coated tongue. Desire for liquor and oranges.

Thirty-sixth day. Dry cough day and night.

Thirty-seventh day. Dry cough on waking. Burning in the hand and all over. Hard and tense pulse. Tongue white in the middle and red at the tip. Pain at the vertex. Sensation as of water splashing in the head. The posterior cervical muscles are stiff. Scarlet-redness of the cheeks. Headache aggravated by work. In bed the sweat smells like potatoes. Tongue very red. Burning hands, with somewhat uneasy pulse.

Thirty-eighth day. The breasts have been painful during the whole time of the proving, the pain is worse when moving the arms, it then seems to become seated at the external border of the pectoralis major. Feels chilly all over, cannot get warm, at half past five in the evening. Scarlet-redness of the cheeks. After dinner, her clothes feel too tight. Dry cough for six minutes, at half past ten in the evening. Her thoughts dwell upon her future, which she imagines will be wretched.

Fortieth day. Dry cough in the evening. Dull colic in the lower abdomen.

Forty-first day. Premature menses. discharge of black coagulated blood. For five days the menstrual blood had a very fetid smell, similar to the smell of spoiled fish. Turbid urine of a dingy yellow, depositing a copious, whitish sediment.

Forty-second day. Burning thirst, as though her mouth were salt. Twitching of the right lower limb. Sensitiveness of the hairy scalp and of the roots of the hairs. Tearing at the vertex; she cannot bear the least covering on her head.

Forty-third day. Hoarseness on rising which disappears

immediately. The same hoarseness in the evening, not long.

Forty-fourth day. Tearing sensation in the throat, with accumulation of phlegm which it is difficult to get loose. Expectoration consisting of yellowish lumps. The phlegm seems to cover the whole anterior portion of the throat. The pain in the throat disappears after talking and stirring about. Sensitiveness of the hairy scalp, every day she feels a pulling in it which does not allow her to bear the comb. In the morning, raising of black, coagulated blood. In the morning she blows bloody mucus from the nose. Nose-bleed every morning, from forty-second to forty-fourth day. She dreams of battles, dead bodies and an immense pool of blood.

Forty-fifth day. She dreams about green men, covered with moss and living in the water; these men were changed to dogs.

Forty-sixth day. At dinner, the dishes taste to her bitter as gall.

Forty-seventh day. Sensation as of some obstacle in her throat which she is unable to expel, followed by the expectoration of a small, hard, yellowish-gray lump. The urine deposits less, though still turbid. When attempting to sing, violent palpitations of the heart prevent her from articulating the sound; her breathing is stopped, she feels as though she would faint. (Her face is scarlet-red).

Fiftieth day. Strong palpitations of the heart, with oppression, and disposition to faint. She is on the point of fainting; a glass of water brings her to.

Fifty-first day. Palpitation of the heart.

Fifty-second day. Heat on the malar eminences and forehead when going out to the open air. Palpitations of the heart, after supper. The palpitation was irregular, stopped for a moment, and then reappeared with redoubled vigour. These palpitations are accompanied by oppressions, less when lying down. Alternate, subcutaneous pulsations or beatings above the knee-pan in the two legs. She does not wish to hear anything in explanation and is out of humour. Red face and congestion of blood to the sclerotica.

Fifty-third day. Palpitation of the heart the whole day. It is caused by the act of swallowing. The palpitation is instantaneous and corresponds to the superior portions of the thorax. (Her lower limbs tremble on account of the hunger).

ARRANGEMENT ACCORDING TO HAHNEMANN

EMOTIVE SPHERE
Quarrelsome, irritable mood, Dread of work. Hypochondriac mood. She wants to enjoy a change of scenery, etc. She fancies she is miserable and dwells much on the future.

SENTIENT SPHERE
Crowd of ideas. His attention is easily disturbed by other things.

HEAD
Heat in the head, evening. Heaviness of the head; in the vertex; on stooping and then raising the head again. Catarrhal dullness of the head, especially the forehead. Headache at noon; increased by the smell of spirits. The head feels too heavy, she has to make an effort to support it. Pressure above the eyes on waking. In the forehead: violent pain all day; stitching pain; with dullness of the head, and disposition to fall forwards. Slight beating in the temples. Sensation as if the hair would be torn out on the vertex.

EYES
Prickling about the lids, the surface of which is red. Spasmodic contraction and twitching of the left upper lid. Burning in the lids. Prickling and burning in the eyes. Congestion of the conjunctiva. Lachrymation on waking.

EARS
Ringing in the left ear.

NOSE
Repeated sneezing, followed by feeble cough. Nosebleed.

FACE
Face hot and red. Mounting of heat to the face, now and then. Upper lip
bleeding, cracked.

TEETH: Swelling of the mucous membrane of the inner margin of the two
incisores. Teeth covered with white mucus.

MOUTH: Dry mouth. Salt taste. Taste of raw potatoes. The mucous
membrane of the velum palati seems to become detached here and there.
Tongue swollen, cracked, early in the morning; coated white or yellowish-
white; or coated white, with red tip, or yellowish along the median line.
Prickling in the right half of the tongue.

THROAT
Inflamed fauces, she is unable to swallow the saliva.

APPETITE
Canine hunger. Food tastes bitter as gall. Great desire for liquor and oranges.

GASTRIC SYMPTOMS
Eructations followed by rumbling in the stomach. Sour eructations causing
a cough. Acidity, bitterness and gulping-up after eating. Cardialgia after
breakfast, dinner and supper.

STOMACH
Pain in the stomach, with red face, after breakfast, spasmodic pains,
griping-tearing at night.

ABDOMEN
Pains and working in the bowels, early in the morning. Painfulness of the
abdomen to contact along the median line. *In the abdomen:* pain after
eating; spasmodic pains, as though the bowels became twisted together; dull
pains in the hypogastric region, at night; pain with chilliness; rumbling; the
clothes cause a feeling of tightness. Emission of flatulence, also with colic.
Pain, as if sprained, in the right groin.

STOOL AND ANUS
Frequent urging to stool. Stool scanty, with straining, passing off in small, black lumps; she has to strain until tears come; hard, large, lumpy; with violent burning in the anus and rectum; hard and large, followed by two liquid stools. Copious, greenish-yellow diarrhœic stool. Constipation for five days. Violent colic previous to stool. Alternate protrusion and retraction of the rectum during stool, with feeling of chilliness in the body.

URINARY ORGANS
Urine reddish, mingled with mucus. Thick urine; it becomes covered with white mucus after standing; turbid, of a dingy-yellow, with copious white sediment; turbid, dingy-yellow, covered with an oily pellicle. Pain in the urethra, after urinating.

SEXUAL PARTS
Weight in the right testicle, the whole day. Suppression of the menses. Menses smelling of foul fish, mixed with black coagula. Small pimples and intolerable itching of the labia. Spasmodic pains striking through the uterus. Burning and itching in the vagina.

WINDPIPE
In the windpipe: tearing, prickling, with cough.Tearing, with phlegm; sensation as of an obstacle, followed by cough and expectoration of a lump of hard, yellowish-gray mucus. Hoarseness, on waking? Cough, with expectoration of yellow mucus at night. Dry cough, day and night. Cough, as from stoppage in the pharynx. Expectoration of lumps of black blood, early in the morning.

CHEST
Constriction and difficulty of breathing, caused by dryness of the mouth. Oppression after supper. Tearing in the chest, also with dryness of the mouth. Sensation, on making the least motion, as though a hollow body were moving about in the chest quickly and with a noise, after which she fancies she will faint, early in the morning. Pricking as from a thousand pins, on the inner surface of the sternum. Violent, stitching pain above the right breast. The mammæ are painful, especially when raising the arm. Congestions to the chest. Acute pain in the left side, like a stitch. Painful stitches in the right

side. Palpitation of the heart, for moments; at night; when lying; when raising one's self; as though the heart would turn; with fainting feeling; with oppression of the chest (less when lying); irregular (after eating).

BACK
Violent beating in the spine, early, when lying. Prickling sensation in the spine, during sleep, waking her. Stinging pain in the large dorsal muscle, right side, when drawing breath. Burning and painful sensation on the fifth dorsal vertebra, caused by the friction of the clothes. Sensation of weariness in the whole back.Stiffness in the muscles of the back. Sense of weight in the back part of the neck. Sensation as if something on the os-sacrum became detached. Pain at the sacrum, when walking or touching the part. Tingling at the os-sacrum. Beating in right shoulder. Prickling in the psoas-muscles. Violent beating in the loins. Pain in the lumbar vertebræ, impeding walking. Intolerable pain in the lumbar region, obliging her to walk bent.

UPPER EXTREMITIES
Feeling of weariness in the muscles, posteriorly. Pain as if sprained, in the right upper arm, after leaning on the elbow. Beating in the middle portion of the triceps brachealis. Heat in the hands. Stinging in the left little finger. Beating in the right ring-finger.

LOWER EXTREMITIES
Acute pains in the hip-joint, caused by the least motion. Painful pressure on the hip-joint as with an iron bar, compelling her to lie down. In the left gluteus muscle: beating; pain, accompanied by loathing. Lancinations in the posterior part of the right thigh. Weary feeling in the muscles of the right side, after walking. Feeling of dislocation in the hip-joint, with pain in the womb, after a slight exertion. Shooting pain in the posterior and inferior femoral muscles, when bending the knee. Beating in the internal femoral muscles. Alternate beating and throbbing above the patella in both limbs. Pain as if sprained, in the whole of the vertebral column, striking through the posterior parts of the thigh and extending down to the heels. Drawing pain in the posterior part of the right lower limb, from the gluteus muscle down to the heel.

GENERAL SYMPTOMS
General and partial debility. Debility, she is about to faint. Weariness in all the limbs, on waking. Pain, as if bruised, in bed, preventing her from stirring. Cold water causes a sense of oppression.

SKIN
Small pimples on the back; causing a violent itching. Small red pimples on the cheeks. The skin in the face peels off a little.

SLEEP
Irresistible drowsiness. Very sleepy in the evening. Restless sleep. Starting from sleep, as in affright. Sleepless. Confused dreams, about fires, revolution, corpses, thieves etc. Amorous dream. He dreams that he is to dress or draw the body of a drowned person, but is prevented in consequence of the body falling all the time on the clothes or paper. Dreams about men who become transformed to talking animals. He dreams that his hands are cut to pieces. He dreams that he is falling from a steeple. She dreams that she is eating human flesh. She dreams that she is swimming in a river, and that she cannot get out of it.

FEVER
Chilliness and sensation of internal coldness. Coldness, with chattering of teeth. Repeated chilly creeping through the whole body in the evening. Feeling of coldness all over, she is unable to get warm, her cheeks being very red, in the afternoon. Heat all over, with sweat. Violent paroxysms of heat, suddenly passing through the whole body and proceeding from the vertex. Alternate, burning heat and chilliness, at night, in bed. Exhalations from the skin, when performing the least work. Sweat all over, early in the morning, in bed. Cold night-sweat. The sweat smells of potatoes in bed. Pulse irritated; irregular, hard and tense.

Benoît Mure

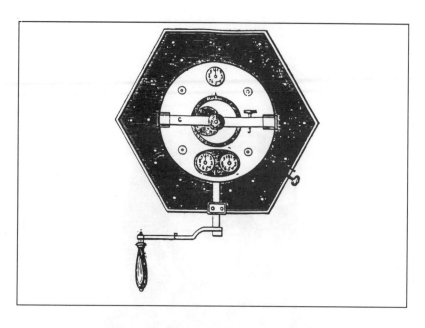

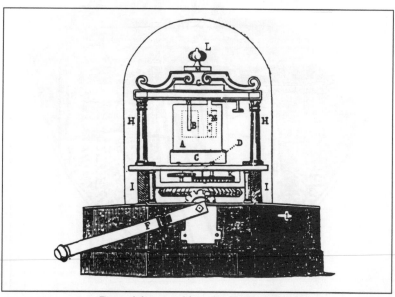

Potentising machines by Benoît Mure

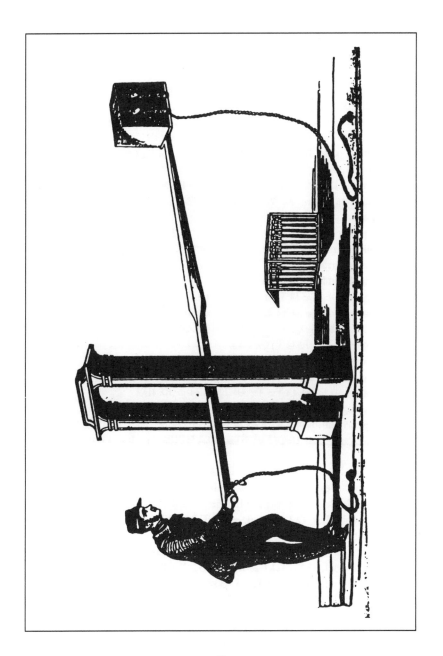

I

Agar. mus. Iωπ Dδ Eλ Tλδ TQπ Fδ Rλ Hδ Bδω Aλ Qπδ YQλ.

Laurocera. Iω Hλ Tδ Yλ Vδ Gλδ Uψ Aλ Rλ.

Platina. Iδπ IYλ Jπλ Mωπδψ Cδλ Gλ Eω Pψ Aλ HTYOFXZδλ.

Mer. per. Lω Jψ Aλ Vδ Bπ Yδ Nμ Mψ Rδ Cλ Hδ.

Opium. p. Iω Jψφ Eψπλ Aπδ Tλπδ Uλ Rλ Fλδ Yλ Oλ Pλ Mδ.

Thea. c. Iπ Jψ Eψλ Tλδ.

Aurum fol. Iδπ JMπ Kπφ HδP⟋ Tπδ Yλ Bπ Nφ Aλ Uδ Mπψ Rλ Lδ.

Belladona. Iωπφ Jλ VJπ Gωπφ Qπφ Tδπ Yπφ Rδλ Vπ Eδ Aδψλ Aπ MYλ.

Elaps cor. Iπλ Jλ Oλ Yλ Rδ Pλ Gφ Eλ Aφ ZXLδλ Qπ Mδ.

Coffea cru. Iω Jπ Qπ Vπ Aπ Dδ Eδ Jδ Tδ Nπ Uψ Xλ.

Natrum carb. Iδ Jλ Qπψ Eπ Hλ Vδ Cδ Aψ Eλ Rφ Mπ Pψ GS⟋ Oλ.

Cannab. ind. Iωψ Jψπ Vπδ Tδ.

Anacard or. Iδπ Jλ Tδ Aλ Mλ Rπλ Hδ.

Solan œgrot. Iπ Jλ Tδ Jφ Aπδ Cλ Vπδ Gωδ.

Petiv. tetr. Iωπλ Jπ Tδ Oλ Jψ Uπ LXZλ Yπ.

Hyos nig. Iπφ Jψλφ TYOλ Gδω.

Ran repens. Iω Jλ Yπ.

Bufo. sa. Iλψ Jψ Yπ Qω Pδ HXZδ Aψ.

Ignat. am. Iδ Mδ Tδ Vπ Yπ Oδ Jψ Aψ Uψ Rλ HKδ.

Ginseng. Iω Qφπ AEδ Hδ Pψ Fπλ Yδ Rλ 1δ Zδ.

Euphorbium. Iψδ Qωπφ Kφ Eλδ YQπ Gπ Dδφ Rπ Tδλ UJπ Aδ Hδ Zψ.

Staphys. d. Iδπ Qπφ Kπδ SVπν Uωδ MPIPλ Pπ Rπ EHλ YQπ Oδ Tδ.

Viola odor. Iω Qψπ Tδ Yδ Oλ Rλ Aδ Uψ Pδ Mω.

Morph. acet. Iω Qψπ Vω Eδλ Tδ Rπ Gωπ Uψ Rδ Yπ Pδ.

Eugenia. Iωπ Tλπδ Bωπ Rπ Hδ Yδπ Aψ Uψ Pψ.

Hydrocia. Iωπ Tλ Cλ Jπλ Rλπ Gλδ Uψ Yδ Vδ Qπ Aλ.

Tabac. n. Iω Tδλ Eδ Uψ Jψ Cλ Rδλ Q⟋∞.

Fluoris acid. Iωπ Uψ Qπφ Mψ Vω Tδ Aλ Rδ HKδ Yω Fδ Oδ.

Sulph. acid. Iλ Vω Aφλ Gφδ Rπ Mψ Uψ Nπ Tδ Yπ.

Natrum sul. Iπδ Vδ Aδ Tδ Hδ Oδ Fδ Gδ Pπ Mψ Rδ HKδ.

Crotalus. Iπλφ Yδ Oλ Gλ Rδ Aδλ HLXZλ⟋ Qφ Vδπ Mδπ.

3 FROM BANTRY TO BEACONSFIELD:
THE REMARKABLE CAREER OF JOSEPH KIDD

I now want to focus directly on a true son of Ireland.[1] Joseph Kidd was born at Limerick in 1824, the seventeenth of eighteen children. His grandfather was a lawyer, and his father a corn merchant, exporting corn through the port of Limerick. His mother came from a Quaker family and Joseph was sent to a Quaker school where he received a good education. He was especially interested in the classics, which he read throughout his life. He helped his father with clerical work in the corn business. At 17 he became an apprentice to a Dr O'Shaughnessy in Limerick. Across the street was another physician who had an apprentice called Quain who acquired a great reputation as an allopath and became quite a celebrity in London in later years.

Dublin

In 1842 he went to Dublin and studied with a Dr Walter who had rooms in Earl Street. He gained experience in dispensing, surgery, home visiting and he appreciated Mrs Walter's cooking. During his free 2 hours each day he studied for the MRCS of England. He studied and worked at the Rotunda, a famous maternity hospital. Here he witnessed a remarkable reduction in the mortality rates created by the simple expedient of securing free ventilation by cutting off the tops of the sash windows so that an open space of 2 feet was left above each window.

---

[1] Walter Kidd, *Joseph Kidd 1824-1918, Limerick London Blackheath; a memoir,* privately printed, 1920, revised 1983

Adventures

Dr Walter is the first homœopath I have discovered in Ireland, but I know little about him. He had been attracted by the principles of homœopathy and his interest in the subject was shared by his pupil, the young Joseph Kidd. Accordingly when a vacancy for a post at the new homœopathic hospital in Hanover Square was advertised in the London *Times* Kidd set off at once to make an application in person for the post, though he was not yet qualified to practice. On his arrival in London he found that 16 qualified men had already applied for the appointment, which was to be filled in a month's time. He applied to the College of Surgeons to be admitted to the next examination for the diploma MRCS which was to take place in three weeks time, but he was told that only 20 candidates could enter at one time and the list was full. Nothing daunted he presented himself at the College on the day of the examination, and finding a student whose courage had failed him at the eleventh hour, he took his place, passed the examination, and shortly afterward his persistence was rewarded, and he was elected house surgeon at the homœopathic hospital.

Curie

At the hospital he worked under Dr Paul François Curie, grandfather of Pierre Curie.[2] So here was his second introduction to the practice of homœopathy.[3] Curie had been brought to England from Paris by a wealthy patron, and set up a poor people's dispensary in the Finsbury area of the city. He wrote a number of books and must have been a positive influence on the young Kidd.[4]

Bantry: the famine

Then came the famine, and Kidd resolved to assist. He was sponsored by the English Homœopathic Society and chose to go to Bantry as being closest to the centres of suffering at Skull and Skibbereen. I have read so

---

[2] John Henry Clarke, *Radium as an internal medicine*, London, Homœopathic publishing Co, 1908 (see dedication)

[3] Paul François Curie, *Domestic homœopathy*, Thomas Hurst, London 1839

[4] Thomas Lindsley Bradford, *Pioneers of homœopathy*, Philadelphia, Boericke & Tafel 1900

many tragic accounts of what he saw that it is hard to know what to give as an example. Kidd wrote a public account,[5] and also a professional one for his colleagues.[6]

Kidd was concerned to show that homœopathy would be effective in the most adverse of conditions where allopathy was ineffective. He had no conception of how adverse those conditions would be. He gladly volunteered to go to Ireland for no material reward and work there as long as he could physically cope. The area of Bantry, Skull and Skibbereen was among the worst affected. People lived in such primitive dwellings as holes in the turf with no floor or furniture. They had sold their clothes to buy food. They lay amid their own excrement and dying or dead families.

He simply took any patient indiscriminately, as they came along. In 67 days he saw 192 patients. He visited them at home and after one week he had as many patients as there was time to visit each day, and the pace carried on. He was only 25 years old and inexperienced. Yet he noticed how the available food, mainly Indian corn imported by the British as aid, was not suitable to help the sick recover so he managed to obtain rice and other better foods from a London voluntary relief agency set up by an alliance of Jews and Quakers.[7]

Dr Kidd's Audit Statistics

Typhus	24
Continued fever	87
total cured	108
	2 died, 1 dismissed
Total	111

---

[5] Joseph Kidd, Homœopathy in acute diseases; narrative of a mission to Ireland during the famine and pestilence of 1847, pages 202-251 in: Marmaduke B Sampson, *Truths and their reception considered in relation to the doctrine of homœopathy*, London, Samuel Highley, for the British Homœopathic Association, 1849

[6] Joseph Kidd, On the fever and dysentery of Ireland in 1847, *British Journal of Homœopathy*, pages 85-109, Volume 6, January 1848

[7] Louis Hyman, *The Jews of Ireland from the earliest times to the year 1910*, London, Jewish Historical Society of England, 1972

mortality	1.8 %
Bantry Hospital mortality	13.5 %
Dysentery	81
	59 cured, 9 better
mortality 14%	11 died, 2 dismissed
Total	162
Bantry Hospital mortality	36%
ages 1-16	48...of which 4 died
ages 16-50	23...of which 3 died
ages 50-70	10...of which 4 died

As Kidd wrote:

> That those under homœopathic treatment, circumstanced as they were in general without proper food or drink, should have succeeded as well as the inmates of the hospital of the same town (taken from precisely the same class of people), with the advantages of proper ventilation, attendance, nourishment etc. would have been most gratifying; but that the rate of mortality under the homœopathic system should have been so decidedly in favour of our grand principle, is a circumstance, it may be hoped, which can scarcely fail to attract the attendance of even the most sceptical.

His figures compared well with the work of other homœopaths working through epidemics all over the world, recorded by the indefatigable librarian of Boericke & Tafel, T L Bradford.[8]

London

After his work in Bantry he returned to London and practised in the City where he was very successful with City men and their wives and families who in those days lived in the City or close by. Over the next few years he attracted patients from all classes and all over the country, setting up another practice in the West End. By 1853 he had graduated MD from King's College Aberdeen. He worked very hard, often arriving early to see poor patients at 7 am before his regular start with paying patients at 9. He also

---

[8] Thomas Lindsley Bradford, *The logic of figures or comparative results of homœopathic and other treatments*, Philadelphia, Boericke & Tafel, 1900

carried out many home visits all over London and the home counties. But he always took holidays ever since a severe illness when he was treated by Drysdale of Liverpool and advised to rest. Thereafter he travelled in Europe every autumn, favouring French, Swiss and Italian resorts. He made his home in Greenwich. He was twice married, first to a Sophia Mackern from Limerick, by whom he had eight children and when he married again Frances Rouse gave him another seven.

It is clear that he began as an avowed homœopath and as the Lancet stated

'he always held fast to the opinion that there is a truth contained in the doctrine of homœopathy which supplies a clue to the treatment of obscure cases.... ...From an early period he adopted the practice of prescribing only one drug at a time so as to be better able to study the action of individual remedies... . ...A large part of his success must be attributed to his careful survey of small details... . ...He trusted little to notes but he seldom forgot a name or an important fact.'[9]

The Laws of Therapeutics

But although he adhered to the rule of similars in his book on the *Laws of Therapeutics*[10] he denied the validity of the infinitesimal dose, decrying Hahnemann for what he perceived as the mysticism of his later years, (rather like Anthony Campbell in his *Two Faces of Homœopathy* one hundred years later).[11]

I learnt for myself that Hahnemann 'sober' teaching the use of the pure undiluted tinctures was a far better guide to heal the sick than Hahnemann drunk with mysticism calling for the exclusive use of infinitesimal doses.

Over this he parted company with the Homœopathic Society.
He had a wide outlook and for example would extend his treatment to

---

[9] Obituary, Joseph Kidd, *The Lancet.*, 21 September 1918
[10] Anthony Campbell, *The two faces of homœopathy,* London, Jill Norman & Hale, 1984
[11] Joseph Kidd, *The laws of therapeutics*, London, C Kegan Paul, 1881

dietary advice, something he learned from his experience in Bantry. He was always ready with a lithographed diet sheet. It was said that he exerted an extraordinary influence on his patients by his personal qualities, tall, handsome, unaffected and sympathetic.

Some of his cases are unremarkable although heroic and well cured, such as *Terebinth* in a urinary problem or *Belladonna* in a throbbing exophthalmic goitre, but here is a neat one which struck Kidd as homœopathic, called:

The influence of a suit of clothes:
A refractory patient at Coney Hatch was in the habit of tearing his clothes into shreds. Mr Tyerman, one of the medical officers, ordered him to be dressed in a brand new suit. The poor man, a tailor by trade, either from a professional appreciation of the value of his new habiliments, or from being touched by this mark of attention, respected their integrity, and from that moment recovered. Before leaving the asylum he stated that he owed his cure to the good effect produced upon his mind by being intrusted with this new suit of clothes.

One of his patients was the reformer John Bright, who remarked that 'not only is he a great doctor, he is also a great philosopher!'

Disraeli

Through his reputation as a homœopath he was cut off from association with the consulting physicians of his day except in the celebrated case of Benjamin Disraeli, the Lord Beaconsfield, his most distinguished patient whom he attended for years.[12]

The first mention was in 1877 when Disraeli wrote in his diary

The only drawback is my health. I really don't see how I can meet Parliament unless some change takes place. It would be impossible for me to address a public assembly. There is no one to consult. Gull, in whom I have little confidence, is still far away, and Dr Kidd, whom all

---

[12] William Flavelle Monypenny & George Earle Buckle, *The life of Benjamin Disraeli, Earl of Beaconsfield*, London John Murray, 1929

my friends wish me to consult, and who of course like all untried men is a magician, won't be in town until the middle of October, and is such a swell that, I believe, he only receives, and does not pay visits – convenient for a Prime Minister!   29 September 1877.

One month later he is really suffering
When I say I am ill, I mean it. I...... am in no degree better, as regards the main and only suffering, asthma. I am now inhaling day and night; a last desperate effort and futile. 25 October 1877,

Today I saw Dr Kidd who cured the Chancellor. I like him much. he examined me as if I were a recruit – but reports no organic deficiency. My main complaint is bronchial asthma, more distressing than bronchitis, but curable where bronchitis is not, and I am to be cured – and very soon!

This is a ray of hope, and I trust I may get to the Lord Mayor's dinner, for if I do not Europe will be alarmed, England agitated, and the Tory party frightened. There is egotism for you!

I had made up my mind never to breathe a word as to my progress or the reverse, until I had given my new man a fair and real trial: but as you press me I can refuse nothing. I will tell you that I entertain the highest opinion of Dr Kidd, and that all the medical men I have known, and I have seen the highest, seem much inferior to him, in quickness of observation, and perception, and reasonableness, and at the same time originality, of his measures. I am told his practice is immense, and especially in chest and bronchial complaints. The difficulty is in seeing him, as he does not like to leave his house.... Nov. 7 1887.

The biographers comment that Kidd afforded Disraeli respite from his malady enabling to appear more frequently in society.

By the next summer, July 1878, Disraeli was engaged in international negotiations and had prevailed upon Kidd to visit him when he was taken ill at the Congress of Berlin! Kidd helped him with asthma and gout and was presented to Bismarck.
Kidd was summoned to relieve Disraeli in Hughenden in January 1879

and regularly for the rest of the winter and the winter of 1880 also.

The final episode in Disraeli's life in 1881 is the subject of differing inter-
pretations by different historians. Monypenny and Buckle are unaware of the
connection with Sir Richard Quain who was called in by the Queen. Victoria
was concerned that Disraeli benefit from the best advice. The connection
was of course that both had been originally apprenticed in the same street in
Limerick. But because Kidd was regarded as a homœopath no doctor would
work with him. '...the regular practitioners were bound by their trade union
rules...'.

Kidd readily agreed to working with Quain. But Quain's consent to attend
was procured by asking Kidd to write that he had not treated his patient
with homœopathy, and that he would follow Quain's advice. (Nowhere in
his posthumous account of Disraeli's illness does Kidd allude to any
controversy). Another physician, Dr Mitchell Bruce from the Brompton
Hospital was called in to relieve Kidd of the night duty. (This was surprising in view of the *Odium Medicum* that ensued a few years later when a
doctor from the Brompton was dismissed for consulting with a homœopath.
The result was a fierce public controversy erupting especially in the *Times*
newspaper, which was subsequently edited into a 126 page book by
Clarke.)[13]

Disraeli died with his left hand in Kidd's saying:
> I have suffered much. Had I been a Nihilist, I should have confessed
> all. I had rather live, but I am not afraid to die.

Dr Kidd revealed his diagnosis after his illustrious patient had died. He
diagnosed Bright's disease in addition to the asthma, which gave him great
trouble, as Beaconsfield would take no exercise save a slow saunter. Kidd
makes much of this refusal to walk at all. Few details are available but Kidd
prescribed *Ipecac, Kali iodatum, Arsenicum,* and lamp baths at various
times.[14] He even suggested Chateau Lafite instead of Port, and generally

---

[13] John Henry Clarke, *Odium medicum and homœopathy: The Times correspondence*
Homœopathic Publishing Company, London 1888

lighter foods. He worked hard at providing a regime which would make Disraeli sweat for he had a dry skin all his life, in order to relieve the kidneys, and he succeeded despite his observation that Disraeli was himself a sharp observer of doctors! "You have conquered" said Disraeli with a genial smile. The morning depression lifted and the albuminuria lessened and freshness and vigour returned.

Dr Kidd

He retained his mental and bodily powers far beyond the ordinary limits of age, and he only retired from practice in his ninetieth year.[15] This man began to follow his medical beliefs when he came to London to become a homœopath. He followed his ethical beliefs when he came back to Bantry as a volunteer in the famine. And then there had been this strangely ironic episode in his career, as he again followed the dictates of his conscience and resigned from the Homœopathic Society over the potency issue and so of course the homœopaths regarded him as an outsider. Yet he worked with the law of similars so the allopaths also regarded him as an outsider! His patients however revered him.

And in the light of his heroic work in Ireland so should we.

---

[14] Joseph Kidd, The last illness of Lord Beaconsfield, *Nineteenth Century,* July 1889
[15] Obituary, Joseph Kidd, *The Times*, 24 August 1918

Dr. Kidd

Dr. Kidd
41

4 HOMŒOPATHY IN ACUTE DISEASES

NARRATIVE OF A MISSION TO IRELAND DURING THE FAMINE AND PESTILENCE OF 1847

By JOSEPH KIDD, Surgeon

There are few patients commencing homœopathic treatment, who do not feel and express their dread of the insufficiency of that treatment in acute disorders or where life is endangered, in their ignorance of the fact, that in none more completely than in the most dangerous diseases does Homœopathy stand successfully over the practice of the old system.

The same objection is also attempted to be made by the greater portion of our medical brethren of the old school, and has been often witnessed in the first trials of the homœopathic principle and medicines by allopathic practitioners, in their transition state from the uncertainty of their former practice, to the true 'rational medicine' of the Homœopathists, founded on a general law which experience proves to be unerring in its guidance, in the proper adaptation of medicine to disease.

To be able to dispel this illusion, it has been ever deemed by the true friends of Homœopathy, most desirable to accumulate evidence, by submitting the system to the most severe and open tests, whenever the opportunity presented itself for applying it in the treatment of acute diseases. It has been felt, indeed, that the success gained in trials of this nature must be the true touchstone of the system, inasmuch as the most favourable results in chronic diseases may always be exposed to special criticism and ingenious explaining away, which writers like Dr. Forbes, confessing the force of the results, but not inclined to give credit to the means, are usually ready to make use of when no other arguments remain.

Thus it is that the full confidence in the truth and universal applicability of the homœopathic principle has ever caused its professors to look with delight on every possible opportunity of testing its actual value as well as in individual cases as in the severest epidemics, whenever and wherever occurring.

The treatment of the epidemic of typhus fever which occurred in Germany in 1813, by Hahnemann himself, is a prominent instance of this kind, when nearly two hundred patients were treated without the loss of a single case, at the time when an enormous mortality attended the mode of practice sanctioned by ages.[1] Again, we have an equally remarkable instance in the promptitude and zeal with which numbers of homœopathic practitioners in Germany, Russia and France, came forward to apply the treatment in the Asiatic cholera, at the last visitation in 1831-2.

Also in various epidemics of scarlatina, measles, etc., treated homœopathically on the continent and in this country, a very interesting account of an epidemic of scarlatina thus treated being contained in the *British Journal of Homœopathy,* Vol. III. p 91, by Dr. Ozanne, of Guernsey, and another of measles, in the January Number of the present year[2] of the same Journal, by the same able practitioner, in both of which remarkable success resulted from the means employed.

As evidence of the same, may be adduced the results obtained in the treatment of acute diseases at the homœopathic hospitals of Vienna and Linz,

---

[1] A most interesting and curious proof of the certainty with which the homœopathic law enables practitioners to apply medicines to any disease may be found in the fact that the medicines used by Hahnemann in 1813, in typhus with such success (*Bryonia* and *Rhus tox*), and by Dr. Quin, of London, in the typhus fever following cholera in Moravia, in 1831, were those which a comparison of the typhus in Ireland with the materia medica enabled me to select, and which my experience found most useful, although ignorant at that time of their use in either of the former cases.

[2] 1848

where the most dangerous diseases have been treated with such success[3] as to have caused the violent remedies of the old system to be laid aside, and to be considered, indeed, positively injurious by many of their former most attached admirers, one of the most celebrated of whom (Skoda, Physician to

---

[3] Comparative results of homœopathic and allopathic treatment in certain acute diseases, furnished by Dr. Fleischmann, of the Homœopathic Hospital at Vienna (from *Introduction to the Study of Homœopathy*, by Drs Drysdale and Russell).

PNEUMONIA (Inflammation of Lungs).
Mortality under ordinary treatment

Authorities	Number of Cases	Deaths
Guisolle	304	43
Briquet	364	85
Edinburgh Infirmary	222	80
Skoda	19	4
Total	909	212

Mortality 23.32 per cent, or nearly one out of four

Mortality under Homœopathic Treatment

Fleischmann	299	19

6.70 per cent, or about one out of fifteen.

PLEURITIS (Inflammation of the lining membrane of Lung).
Mortality under ordinary treatment
Authorities

Edinburgh Infirmary	111	14

12.61 per cent, or about one out of eight.

Mortality under Homœopathic Treatment

Fleischmann	224	3

1.24 per cent, little more than one out of a hundred

PERITONITIS (Inflammation of the lining membrane of the Cavity of Abdomen and of Intestines).
Mortality under ordinary treatment

Edinburgh Infirmary	21	6

27.61 per cent or more than one out of four

Mortality under Homœopathic Treatment

Fleischmann	105	5

4.76 per cent, or less than one out of twenty-five.

the General Hospital at Vienna,) now regards 'hay water' as the best and universal medicine for all diseases. Finally, perhaps, the same confidence in the truth and universal applicability of the homœopathic system may be found in the results of its trial in the epidemic of fever and dysentery in Ireland, in 1847, undertaken by myself, at the request of the committee of the English Homœopathic Association, and carried out in the face of difficulties and dangers not to be surmounted, save by a firm confidence in the unvarying truth of the homœopathic law.

As introductory to our more immediate object, a glance at the history of the great Irish famine of 1846-7, will be necessary.

Ireland has been visited, from time to time for centuries, with partial and almost periodical famines,[4] which except as matters of history, and for the suffering produced in the localities afflicted, were soon lost sight of, and their sad but instructive lessons unheeded. Few of the present generation will ever forget the melancholy visitation of 1846-7, when, at the approach of some unseen but all-powerful agent, of which we know exactly nothing, the food of millions of human beings was destroyed in the course of a very few days,[5] and when in the face of the most amazing efforts made for its relief

---

[4] In the year 1740-1 (called the year of slaughter), it was estimated that one-fifth of the entire population perished of want and fever! In the years 1798 to 1800, general scarcity and dearness of all provisions. In 1817-8, general distress all over Ireland, from the same causes, one million and a half of the population having been affected with fever that year. In 1822, almost total loss of the potato crop in Munster and Connaught. In 1831, the same in Galway, Mayo and Donegal. In 1835-6-7, partial famine in various parts of Ireland. In 1839 a partial failure of the potato crop in most parts of Ireland.

[5] The following extract from the able and impartial history of the 'Irish crisis,' by Mr. Trevelyan, in the *Edinburgh Review* (January 1948) conveys a good description of the rapid destruction of the potato crop which then took place: "On the 27th of last month (July), I passed," Father Matthew writes in a letter published in the parliamentary papers, "from Cork to Dublin, and this doomed plant bloomed in all the luxuriance of an abundant harvest. Returning on the 3rd instant (August), I beheld with sorrow one wide waste of putrefying vegetation. In many places the wretched people were seated on the fences of their decaying gardens, wringing their hands, and wailing bitterly at the destruction that had left them foodless."

45

by all classes of society in England, America and various continental coun-tries, hundreds of thousands of victims told how insufficient all human aid must prove at such a crisis.

The recent potato disease first appeared in Ireland in the autumn of 1845, and caused the destruction of a large portion of that season's crop, but only in particular districts, and to a partial extent, which was in some degree compensated for by an abundant crop of corn and green vegetables, hay etc., so that none were prepared for the universal destruction of the next year's crop, which occurred much earlier in the season (long before vegetation had ceased), and more generally than at the previous visitation. The corn crops also proved very deficient, both in those countries, and all over Europe, necessarily followed by an extraordinary increase in prices, so that in most parts of Ireland the cost of provisions became more than doubled, and in many places (where food at other times was cheapest) nearly trebled. The almost inevitable consequences soon followed; the greater part of the population, previously existing – almost without the use of money – on potatoes, easily obtained by a small outlay of labour and seed, found them-selves without food, or the means of purchasing it, and want and starvation began to prevail very generally. At this particular juncture, the system of 'public works' was humanely instituted by the Government, afterwards so grievously abused, and gradually extended during the winter and spring, till the major portion of the male population was employed.[6]

As the winter advanced, distress increased to a most fearful extent, in spite of the employment given to myriads of the people, and melancholy instances of death from actual starvation were of daily occurrence by the roadsides, in the fields, and often of entire families, shut up in their wretched hovels. Thus did matters go on without improvement till the latter end of March, when vast supplies of Indian corn and meal arriving from America, and the

---

[6] The numbers were – in October, 114,000, in December, 440,000, in January, 570,000 thence gradually increasing till March when 734,000 (representing nearly three millions of the population) were so employed, when the Government found it necessary to dismiss twenty per cent, and the remainder gradually, till nearly all were disbanded in June, as otherwise the lands would have remained uncultivated.

continent,[7] prices declined most rapidly, and the supply, even in the most backward places became abundant, from which time the previously numerous instances of death by starvation became more and more rare, finally disappearing as the system of out-door relief under the new Poor-Law Act came into operation, towards June and July.

As might have been expected, disease rapidly followed in the track of famine,[8] adding fresh victims to the ravages of the latter, prolonging (or renewing) the period of suffering and affliction.

Dysentery had appeared early in that fearful winter, increasing in amount until spring (the time most to be dreaded for epidemics), when fever followed, and the entire of Ireland became covered with a widely-devastating pestilence, by which numbers of the clergymen of all persuasions, medical men and the resident gentry, who had devoted themselves to the relief of their afflicted fellow-creatures, fell victims to their benevolent exertions.[9]

I cannot better illustrate the ravages which fever and dysentery were then committing, than by introducing the following quotation from the second edition of my friend Mr. Sampson's work on Homœopathy,[10] published in January of the present year, which will at the same time explain the cause and origin of my mission to Ireland.

---

[7] In the last week of March, it was estimated that in the harbour of Cork alone, upwards of 250 vessels were lying, containing nearly 50,000 tons of Indian corn, and a fall in price of three to four pounds a ton took place within a few weeks. - The Irish crisis, in *Edinburgh Review*, January 1848.

[8] The connection between famine and fever will be resumed in another place.

[9] The week after my arrival in Bantry, the Rev. Dr. Trail, of Skull (10 miles from Bantry), died of exhaustion, consequent upon repeated attacks of the epidemic, caught in close attendance upon his poor parishioners: also Capt. Drury, the inspecting officer of public works in Kinsale; and the curate of Bantry (Rev. A. Hallowell), as well as the physician to the Union, were both laid up with the same disease; also one or two Roman Catholic priests, in the county between Bandon and Cork.

[10] Marmaduke B Sampson, *Homœopathy its Principle, Theory, and Practice*, London, Samuel Highley, 1848

During the early part of 1847, the accounts from Ireland of the daily extending ravages of pestilence first took that frightful form, which caused the year to assume that place it now occupies in the records of human calamity. It was not, however, until the 26th of March that the extent of the evil became fully known. On that day the news came from three localities widely asunder, Armagh, Mayo and Cork, that the progress of disease in the respective districts was such, that hundreds of the sufferers were without any medical assistance whatever, that the workhouses were crowded and that the attendants and medical men were daily dying, so that, in many instances, both paupers and officers were alike destitute.

'In Ballinrobe,' said the *Mayo Constitution* of the 23rd of March, 'the workhouse is in the most awfully deplorable state, pestilence having attacked nearly all within its walls. In fact, the building is one horrible charnel-house, the unfortunate paupers being nearly all the victims of a fearful fever, the dying and the dead, we might say, huddled together. The master has become one of the victims; the clerk, a young man, whose energies were devoted to the well-being of the Union, has been added to the number; the matron too, is dead, and the respected and esteemed physician has likewise fallen, in his constant attendance on the deceased inmates. This is the position of the Ballinrobe house, every officer swept away, while the number of deaths amongst the inmates is unknown. It yet remains, also, to add, that the Roman Catholic chaplain lies dangerously ill of the same epidemic.

From Cork the accounts were equally alarming, and amongst other details, mostly showing that 'professional men seemed to be more particularly marked out as doomed victims of the malady,' and that, consequently, the great want amongst the mass of the sufferers was that of medical attendance, the following appeared in the Reporter newspaper:

Most horrible – most dreadful – are the last accounts from the west of Cork, even to listen to the description given by eye-witnesses of what is passing in that part of our county, and, above all, in the two Carberies. A gentleman who has sojourned there, whose duties compelled his stay, assured us no later than last Sunday, that none of the communications appearing in our journal conveyed an adequate notion of the terrible realities. It is not food the unfortunate people now want most – it is medical attendance; not additional poorhouses, but hospitals they require. A pestilential fever, more mortal and destructive than cholera or plague, is carrying off the poor. All the food, solid or liquid, on earth could not save them without medicinal and sanitary accompaniments of the most extensive, active, and efficient sort. There is not a house from Bantry to Skull, that, with scarce a dozen exceptions, does not contain either the sick, the dying or the dead. The latter lie where they die, or are barely pushed outside the thresholds, and there suffered to dissolve. Their living relatives within the huts are too feeble to remove them further; and the strong, outside, from distant places (and they indeed are few) are afraid to handle unshrouded and uncoffined bodies. Judge of the consequences. The weather begins already to grow warm, and decomposition sets in more rapidly than a month since. Let us state two or three facts which we have on unimpeachable testimony. Our informant is one who, besides being incapable of an untruth, has an interest rather in exposing than encouraging exaggeration. He has told us, that in one locality, where public works are in progress, the labourers were forced to examine a cabin at some distance, in consequences of the noxious and intolerable effluvium issuing from it. They discovered in it five bodies in an advanced stage of putrefaction, the whole of a family who had died none knew when. None of the labourers dared touch the bodies, and to protect themselves while remaining on the work, where they were compelled to earn their bread and chance of life, they pulled down the hovel, heaped timber and thatch over the blackened corpses, applied fire, and kept aloof until the dwelling and the dead were consumed to ashes. Such was the internment.[11] It is our duty to publish these appalling facts. We haveauthentic information of others just as dreadful, but our flesh creeps at the remembrance. We must, however, in order if possible to instigate the authorities to adopt proper measures, state one other fact for their consideration. In the neighbourhood of Dunmanus Bay three dead bodies were lying for many days, and still, we believe, remain exposed outside the thresholds of three cabins,

---

[11] (Cremation was not then a normal method of disposal of the dead, and at least among Catholics was forbidden until very recently; Ed)

while within, the families were dead, or dying, or struck down by fever. None of the peasantry, for the world's wealth, would go near the bodies – such is their apprehension of contagious fever; even the Water Guards at a neighbouring station dreaded to approach them. There they lay, festering in the sun, and breeding pestilence, and there for aught we know, they still remain, emitting poisonous exhalations, and rendering the recovery of the sick within the cabins altogether hopeless.

When these accounts, which appeared in the Times of the 26th of March first met the eye of the author of the present work, the idea instantly flashed upon him, that a more noble field on which to test the powers of Homœopathy could not have been presented. He accordingly requested Mr. Heurtley, the Honorary Secretary of the English Homœopathic Association, with which he and that gentleman were then connected, to summon a meeting of the Committee, with the view of proposing that a homœopathic practitioner should be immediately despatched, at the expense of the Association, to the scene of destitution, with instructions for him to proceed at once to Bantry or Skibbereen, or whichever might prove the most infected district, and there to offer his gratuitous aid, without any other limit than that which would be occasioned by the exhaustion of his own physical powers. This proposal was at once hailed by the Committee, and after an attempt at opposition from two persons whose motives subsequently transpired, and from whom the leading friends of Homœopathy have subsequently disconnected themselves, it was immediately adopted and carried into execution. The party selected for the arduous mission was Mr. Joseph Kidd, an Irishman, but a member of the London College of Surgeons, and this gentleman joyfully undertook its duties without the slightest prospect of remuneration, and in the full consciousness of all the appalling circumstances with which he would be called upon to contend. He knew that in the midst of the ordinary difficulties of his task he would be assailed by the cries for food of the miserable beings by whom he would be surrounded, that he would have to attend the sick lying side by side with the dead, that all ordinary requirements would be disregarded, that fresh air, warmth, cleanliness and every other aid would be wholly wanting, that he could hope for no professional co-operation, and that, in fact, it would have been difficult to have imagined circumstances of greater disadvantage under which his exertions could be carried on. But he had had some years' experience of Homœopathy, and hence he went with undaunted confidence upon what, under other circumstances, would have seemed a hopeless and a most dangerous undertaking.

This very serious step was undertaken by me, not in a spirit of blind enthusiasm, but after the most mature consideration of all the dangers, obstacles and difficulties which might be expected to oppose our efforts, and in the full confidence that at all times Homœopathy wants nothing but a field in which it may be tested, to prove triumphant.

Nor was my confidence shaken even by the gloomy forebodings and discouraging opposition of a professional colleague, who was at that time a leading member of the Committee of the Association, nor by the petty and vexatious impediments of another professional member, belonging to that 'genus irritabile' whose love of approbation preponderating over the intellectual faculties, cause them to view an original idea of any other mind, no matter how beautiful and perfect, as if it were unsightly, and to oppose it by every petty shift and hindrance in their power.[12]

Leaving London on the night of Saturday, April 3rd, with the utmost dispatch, the following Tuesday found me in the city of Cork, and, after making the necessary enquiries, I determined to press forward to some part of the west of the county of Cork, where most disease and destitution were reported to exist. Accordingly, I started for Bandon, where I called upon the rector (the Hon. and Rev. Mr. Bernard), who very kindly afforded me much information about the state of the country, and recommended me most earnestly to make Bantry the scene of operations, knowing it to be then over-flowing with disease, and that, on account of the illness of its chief physician, and the increase of sickness, it was, in a great degree, destitute of medical aid.

---

[12] It is deserving of remark, that no sooner had the idea thus opposed led to success-ful results, than the party last alluded to took immediate occasion to attempt the appropriation of a portion of the credit of the scheme, and to bruit about the share of *eclat* due to him, for his exertions in having urged it on.

Without loss of time, therefore, I went forward, and reached Bantry towards midnight, where the sounds of misery soon came upon our ears from the sobbing crowds of children at the coach windows, as, drenched with rain, they importuned for food. Never was a more pitiable cry raised; and by those upon whom it fell, it can scarcely ever be forgotten.

Bantry is a small town in the west of the county Cork, with a population of about 5000, situated near the bay of that name; and within a few miles of those places, immortalised in the annals of suffering and distress, Skibbereen and Skull. The country surrounding it forms the most picturesque and grand district in the south-west of Ireland.

Immediately after my arrival in Bantry, I called upon the vicar, (the Rev. John Murphy), whose kindness was most liberally extended to me in many ways, during my entire stay, and the example of whose devotion to the relief of his destitute parishioners of all sects became a continual source of encouragement to me in my labours in the same field. This gentleman forthwith invited me to accompany him on one of his daily visits of charity, through the outskirts of the town, and then for the first time did the full reality and extent of the desolation of the people come upon my astonished vision. Up to this period I had only seen, in my rapid passage through the country, a few of the ordinary horrors of the times; and as we visited one after another, the wretched huts filled to overflowing with disease and misery in the most loathsome and terrible condition to which human nature could be reduced, I found how far even imagination had fallen short of what was really to be witnessed.

For months previously I had read, in common with everybody else, the sickening details of the sufferings of those poor people in the English and Irish journals. I had read of them until the whole thing seemed a mass of exaggeration, drawing the crowding horrors of all other centuries into one hapless period and locality. Even, however, with all this, and the glimpses of misery I had caught since my arrival in Cork, I was totally unprepared for the ghastly sights which encountered us at every step.

In a very short time we saw some hundreds of cases of fever and dysentery lying in the most helpless and destitute condition. In many of the wretched huts, every inmate lay abandoned to their fate. Fever and dysentery side by side on the same scanty pile of decomposing straw, or on the cold earthen floor, without food or drink. In a few cases we saw fever patients exposed under the lee of houses or walls, half protected from the inclemencies of that climate (proverbially a moist one) by a few furze bushes. Entering one house, our eyes met the coffins with sliding bottoms,[13] which it had been found necessary to introduce, and which in this instance were employed to remove two of four victims to fever in one family, having been used for the others a few days previously, leaving two more almost in a lifeless condition in the midst of the same virulent disease.[14]

I communicated that night with Mr. Heurtley, the Honorary Secretary, apprising him of what I had witnessed, and stating that very little chance existed of any systematic plan of operation being carried out. It was therefore resolved that I should devote my services promiscuously wherever they might be most needed. Accordingly, each succeeding day found me alone amongst some of the most wretched of those that I had recollected seeing on my first survey, and after much trouble in each case, even in procuring vessels to contain the medicine, and loss of time in cleansing them myself, I was enabled to leave what was most appropriate. Thus did matters go on, gradually increasing the number of cases (every one of which was carefully entered in a notebook), till it reached nearly a hundred, before the end of a week.

By degrees the sphere of operations enlarged, till, to visit one half of the entire number under treatment, became a hard day's work, requiring me to be out from ten or eleven o'clock in the morning till five, six or seven in the afternoon, the greater part of which time was spent in the most intimate

---

[13] Owing to the enormous increase of mortality at Bantry, and several other places, it became almost impossible to procure coffins for the dead, which obliged the Relief Committee to have coffins made with moveable bottoms. Horses and men were employed to carry the dead in these coffins to the graveyard, *where they were buried* in large pits, one of which, it is stated, contained nearly 500 bodies, before it was closed in June or July, all of whom had died in the workhouse alone.

[14] These two were amongst the first cases whose treatment I undertook. It will be seen from the note of cases 7 and 8 in the Appendix that they both recovered. (See illustration)

contact with fever and dysentery, being frequently obliged to remain nearly half an hour in one single hovel, crowded with poor sufferers, till human nature could hold out no longer, and an instinctive and almost convulsive effort would cause me to escape from the close atmosphere of peat-smoke and fever-miasm to the open air.

At the conclusion of the day's work, with face, hands and clothes begrimed with smoke and dirt, would I reach home, with the same ordeal to pass through on the morrow, and every day; and yet, notwithstanding such exposure to the most fruitful sources of contagion, I escaped most perfectly, although the only precautions observed were, an hour's walk every morning over the hills of that beautiful country, and moderation in living.

I shall now proceed with the history, description and treatment of fever and dysentery in Bantry, in so far as it fell under my observation.

The history of fever, as it appeared in Ireland during the spring and summer of 1847, is highly interesting in its medical relations and also in the very important and instructive lessons of political economy, deducible from the very close connection which it has proved to exist between famine and fever.

A warm controversy has been carried on as to this connection by two very able physicians in Dublin. Dr. Corrigan, of the Whitworth and Hanwick Fever Hospitals, and my friend Dr. H, Kennedy, of the Cork Street Fever Hospital. The former published a pamphlet in 1845,[15] ascribing the production of fever to the direct agency of famine, strengthening his assertion by many telling facts and coincidences collected from the histories of previous epidemics. This opinion was also very much favoured by the epidemic of the next year following immediately on the great famine of that year. Dr Kennedy, however, in his pamphlet,[16] published the year after Dr. Corrigan's,

---

[15] *On Famine and Fever, as Cause and Effect in Ireland, with Observations on Hospital Location, and the Dispensation in Outdoor Relief of Food and Medicine.* By D. J. Corrigan, M.D., M.R.C.S.E.

[16] *Observations on the Connection between Famine and Fever in Ireland and elsewhere.* By H. Kennedy, M.B., A.B., T.C.D.

giving the matter a more searching and philosophical examination, contro-
verts the position of the former, proving from numerous examples, and from
the late visitation, that the amount of famine bore no relation to the amount
of fever, that famine often occurred without fever, and vice versa, and that
in some cases, famine existed for a long time without fever, and soon after
abundance had replaced it that fever then broke out with great virulence. He
also pointed out that several epidemics of fever in Ireland were ascribed by
their historians to superabundance of food; and the conclusions he arrived at
were, that there is a very intimate connection between famine and fever, not
as cause and effect, but as effects of one and the same cause, 'the epidemic
constitution,' which, affecting the vegetable world, had caused the destruction of food, and which, in the human family, had produced fever and other
epidemic diseases. His arguments are, that the epidemic tendency to fever
and various other diseases (small-pox, scarlatina etc.) had commenced
before the famine, that these epidemic diseases had in most cases extended
into other countries, far removed from the seat of famine; and that the same
influence had also affected the lower animals with peculiar diseases.

Fever became prevalent in Bantry and its neighbourhood in the beginning
of February, and continued to increase till the end of May, when it commenced to decline, both in frequency and in virulence, the amount in June
being considerable, while in July and August a most rapid diminution took
place, amounting indeed, almost to a total disappearance.[17]

The causes of fever have been generally divided into predisposing and
exciting,[18] the former being those which induce or cause changes in the
system (as improper and insufficient food, by lowering the general standard
of health and causing depression of the mind and spirits), that render the

---

[17] Fever and dysentery have been again prevalent there this year, but to a slight
degree, compared with the previous year.

[18] Predisposing causes have been also named internal, or belonging to the system, that
is, that the changes produced in the conditions of the solids and fluids of the body
and of the *moralé* of the mind by those causes, are the true predisposing causes, and
not their direct agency. Exciting causes have also been named *external*, their agency
being *direct*, and from without (as contagion or exposure to cold and wet).

individual more susceptible of the disease, when exposed to an exciting cause; the latter, those which actually induce or engender the disease.

The principal of the predisposing causes my be considered mental and physical depression, the results of improper and insufficient food, over fatigue or anxiety, sudden changes of temperature, the ordinary changes of seasons and the crowding together of many individuals in close, ill-ventilated rooms,[19] where the light of the sun is entirely or partially excluded.

The principal exciting causes of fever may be enumerated as, contagion (by contact or communication with others previously affected), emanations from animal or vegetable matter in a state of decomposition and exposure to cold or wet.

These causes (both predisposing and exciting) operate with different force and in different proportion in different epidemics, the most powerful in one being often absent in another; as an invariable rule, the more of them in operation, and the longer the time of that operation, the greater probability that fever will follow. In the epidemic which constitutes the immediate object of the present Essay, few will deny that famine, with its long train of secondary consequences, was the most powerful and constant of the predisposing causes, while of the exciting causes, the most active were contagion and exposure to cold and wet.

In the condition of the people at Bantry, and places similarly afflicted, every circumstance favourable to the development of fever could be observed; in the crowding together [20] of numbers of debilitated individuals

---

[19] In some instances this would seem to become a direct or exciting cause , as in that of 'the black hole' at Calcutta, where fever attacked every one of the survivors *directly*; also in the sudden crowding on board emigrant and convict ships, in gaols etc.
[20] Owing to the number of poor people obliged to desert their dwellings in the country parts (where starvation threatened), to seek refuge in the town, all the huts became filled to suffocation with occupants, (three, four or five families occasionally living in one house or room) in which fever was sure to break out, of a most dangerous and fatal character.

in the lowest state of mental and physical depression, in most cases existing upon one small meal (containing from six to eight ounces of solid nourishment) each day, for which they were obliged to remain in a state of semi-nakedness,[21] exposed under the open air in a dense crowd surrounding the soup kitchen (where many scarcely recovered from fever were forced to come) for eight, ten or twelve hours,[22] owing to the difficulty and delay in preparing cooked food for so many thousands.

The most prevailing type of fever in Bantry was continued fever; there was also a good deal of typhus with extreme nervous depression and debility; also some cases of inflammatory typhus with furious delirium, raving and other evidences of cerebral implication.

Continued fever generally commenced (in most cases after exposure to contagion) with languor, muscular exhaustion and mental depression with headache after a few days becoming more thoroughly developed, with increase in frequency of pulse, (although the strength and volume were very deficient) dryness and heat of skin, heaviness and dull aching pain over the frontal region in the eyes and eyelids, constant thirst with dryness of mouth, white, brownish or yellow coating of the tongue, loss of appetite, nausea, vomiting with painful sensibility of the epigastrium, constipation, urine in general very little changed in quality, rather deeper in colour but without deposit and scanty. In many cases chest symptoms appeared, with cough of various characters, either dry and hard, with thick whitish phlegm, difficult of expulsion, with or without pricking pains in the chest on coughing, or full

---

[21] Early in the course of the distress, there was a universal rush amongst the people to pledge and dispose of their clothes to procure food, insomuch that every pawn-broking establishment in that entire country became suddenly filled, so that their capital being expended, they were ultimately obliged to remain idle or closed for many months; necessarily, the sufferings of the poor from the loss of their clothes, when the severe weather appeared, were incalculable.

[22] Often have I seen a large portion of the crowd unserved with their scanty pittance at ten, eleven or even twelve o'clock at night, occasionally obliged to leave without it till the next day; it was a matter of perfect certainty that most of those remaining even to that time had not tasted food of any sort since the corresponding hour the day (or night) previously.

and shaking, with copious, thick, yellowish-white expectoration. In some cases the cough was attended with obstruction of breathing and thick, tenacious, muco-sanguineous expectoration and dull or acute pains in the chest.

Almost invariably in the early stages of this variety of fever, appeared aching or shooting pains in the extremities (mostly in the lower), aggravated by movement, and attended with tenderness and pain in the muscular portion of the limbs; the sleep was generally disturbed at night, either by the teasing cough setting in towards midnight, or by general anxiety and restlessness.

The first symptom of amendment was generally seen in diminution of the frequency of pulse, gradually followed by amelioration of the pains in the head and limbs, in the cleaning of the tongue around its edges, returning appetite, softness and coolness of skin and sleep, till convalescence became established (about the sixteenth to twentieth day).

The medicines used by me in the treatment of this class of fever cases were *Aconite, Bryonia* and *Belladonna.* In many cases, towards the middle and later stages, it was found necessary to administer *Nux vomica*; in some cases, also, *Rhus toxicodendron* was resorted to. Several other medicines were used in isolated cases, and against particular symptoms.

The approach and progress of typhus differed very much from continued fever; from the very commencement the heat of skin and acceleration of pulse being very inconsiderable, and in the middle and latter stages being almost invariably below the natural standard. For two or three days the patient would labour under lassitude and languor, with loss of appetite and of sleep, the tongue being generally the first index of the probable mischief in store. About the fourth or fifth day the disease being generally well marked with a very slight heat of skin, which felt soft and clammy, being covered with moisture, (not like the ordinary feel of a perspiring skin, but as if the skin were damped and by some contrivance all evaporation prevented) the pulse very little, if at all altered, except in strength, which even at this period would be somewhat deficient; the tongue presented a most characteristic appearance, in general dry, hard and glazed. like brown leather, or deeply covered with brown or blackish fur. In some cases it appeared soft, moist and tremulous, covered with a perfect and uniform layer of pure white paste or mucus, (this in general omened a very severe and dangerous form of the disease) the gums and teeth become covered with brownish incrustations, thirst being incessant and insatiable, with nausea and vomiting; in many cases abdominal symptoms, as tension and tympanitic resonances of abdominal wells, with tenderness and shooting pain over either iliac region (in general the right); bowels seldom costive, in general relaxed, with or without pain; urine in a few cases suppressed, in most unchanged; head in general implicated, in most from the beginning, with aching and heaviness at the forehead, throbbing at the temples, vertigo, sense of emptiness and bewilderment; delirium, mostly at night, with low muttering or with stupid heavy insensibility, and incoherence of speech.[23] The eyes appeared, dull, inanimate and listless, with the head instinctively turned from the light. In a few cases, towards their termination, a peculiar sort of stolid deafness supervened, which gradually disappeared as convalescence advanced.

Almost invariably, the lower extremities were complained of as being dead and numbed, rendering the least motion impossible (but without any actual pain), the feet and legs feeling cold and damp.

General debility and prostration set in early in the disease and proved the most obstinate of the symptoms.

In most cases sleep was disturbed or absent for many days and nights, with general restlessness, frequently caused by teasing cough, most usually coming on about midnight. In a few cases the cough was attended with obstruction of breathing, and sharp or dull pains in the chest, or with abundant mucous expectoration, which the patient had much difficulty in expelling.

The first symptoms of improvement generally appeared about the fourteenth or fifteenth day, in the condition of the tongue, the dry glazed appearance becoming interspersed with patches of moist redness, and the

---

[23] Where consciousness existed in this period, there was great mental anxiety and depression with restlessness and want of sleep.

uniform white paste-like layer breaking off in flakes, exposing the natural pale-red appearance of the tongue below. Gradually sleep visited the sufferer, appetite returned and convalescence ensued with tolerable rapidity and was very well established in fifteen days after the improvement commenced.

The medicines chiefly used in typhus were *Rhus tox., Bryonia, Arsenicum* and *Phosphorus*; *Aconite* being seldom employed except in a few cases where the treatment commenced very early or where heat and dryness of skin existed for a few days. In most cases it was not found necessary at any period of the disease, the sphere of operation and utility of *Aconite* in typhus being very small compared with that in continued fever.

The medicines upon which most reliance were placed, and which proved most successful, were the four already enumerated, although some others were used in a few cases.

The convalescence of the fever patients was most satisfactory, indeed too rapid in most of the cases of continued fever, as the poor sufferers, finding their strength to be so quickly restored, were apt to make too free with the cold air, and to partake largely of indigestible food (Indian meal, in hard cakes or in porridge, even rice in many cases proving too indigestible), the result of which was that nearly one-sixth of all the cases of continued fever suffered a relapse[24] to a fever of far worse character although of shorter duration than the original. This generally occurred about the second or third day after all traces of the original fever had disappeared, and in most instances the one single cause (improper food) could be traced, which the first glance at its symptoms immediately confirmed. In a few, exposure to cold in the open air, or to draughts of cold air in their houses, proved the exciting cause.

Every possible effort was made to guard against this disagreeable consequence, by restraining the patients to bed, or to the room, as long as a symptom of fever remained and by giving careful directions as to diet, also by explaining the dangerous nature of the relapse fever; but in many cases

---

[24] The same unusually great liability to relapse had been previously noticed in several epidemics of fever folowing famine in Ireland.

(as might naturally have been expected) without avail, as convalescents after fever generally feel a very sharp appetite for the first few weeks, to restrain which would have required more philosophy and reasoning powers than those wretched creatures could be supposed to have possessed, particularly at such a time, with the dread of actual starvation impending over them.

The food found to agree best with convalescents was rice, boiled in water, or milk (rarely); in some cases white bread and milk, boiled or not. These, however were obtainable in a very small number of instances.[25] With few exceptions, therefore, the cases I had dealt with were again taken under the treatment. In the detailed results, however, which will be found in Appendix, these are not entered as fresh cases, and the double cure, therefore, is merely recorded as a single one.

The symptoms of the relapse fever were in general throbbing, shooting pains in the forehead and at the top of the head, with vertigo, flushing of face, expressive of intense anxiety, restlessness and despair of recovery, the eyes looking dull and inanimate, with quivering of the eyelids, the tongue presenting one almost unvarying character, being soft, moist, tremulous and covered with a dense layer of whitish fur or paste, nausea, sickness, and vomiting, frequently to a most distressing extent, with soreness at the epigastrium, aggravated by food, drink or pressure, bowels generally relaxed, with griping pains, or constipated, skin burning hot and moist, pulse rather accelerated, but weak or irregular, constant agitation and restlessness, with loss of sleep. The usual duration of the relapse fever was from four to

---

[25] Towards the close of my labours in Bantry, the humane exertions of Mr. Sampson enabled me to obviate this melancholy want, the Committee of the 'British Association for the Relief of the Destitute in Ireland,' having through his representations placed a quantity of rice at my disposal. His Grace, the Archbishop of Dublin at the same time transmitted me, through the same channel, a donation of £10, and Mr. Samuel Jones Loyd a like amount. I also received £2 from Richard Beamish, Esq., F.R.S., the whole being for the relief of the destitute convalescents. This enabled me, as my professional exertions were coming to a conclusion, to provide with rice, bread and milk, and fuel, many hundreds, partly those who had recovered under my own care, and every one else that seemed in the same condition after sickness, that I could make out, that otherwise might have perished from imperfect convalescence, diarrhœa and want.

eight days, when the nausea and pain at the epigastrium diminished and the tongue became clean, with gradual disappearance of the other symptoms.

Nux vomica was found to be the most certain and useful medicine in these cases, (sometimes preceded by a few doses of *Aconite*) under its action the tongue becoming rapidly clean, the skin cool and the headache disappearing, so that in a few days the patient was again in a fair way towards recovery, but with an increased degree of weakness. It was generally administered every four hours, in solution in water (the tincture), the intervals being gradually lengthened to twelve or twenty-four hours. *Bryonia* and *Arsenicum* were also used.

Two or three cases suffered a second relapse and were again treated with success. There were instances even of a third relapse.

Relapse followed typhus much less frequently, in proportion to the number of cases than continued fever, which happy immunity was principally owing to the return of strength being more gradual, and the appetite not being so soon restored, which rendered the convalescents more careful in taking food, and in going into the open air.

Where relapse did follow typhus, it approached more closely in character to the original fever than did the relapse of continued fever to its original type, and, as might have been expected, with an increased degree of debility and exhaustion, which rendered it more dangerous and fatal than ordinary typhus; one of the two deaths from fever being in relapse after typhus (the second was in a case of continued fever with pleuro-pneumonia).

As health became restored to the convalescents and as they reverted to their old mode of diet, diarrhœa frequently followed, particularly after typhus, or where much debility had previously existed; it was most usual in old persons, or in young from about the ages of six to sixteen years. From the utter impossibility of removing the exciting cause in most cases, it generally proved a tedious and distressing complaint; at one time being almost cured, but again breaking out, as the cause came into more active operation.

The medicines used were *Arsenicum* in the commencement, and *Rhus, China, Secale* etc., in the latter stage.

As another of the sequelæ of fever, dropsical effusion into the cellular tissue occurred most frequently after typhus and often to a very great extent. It usually appeared the first week after the convalescence had been established. *Phosphorus, Bryonia, Rhus* and *China* were the medicines generally used.

DYSENTERY

The principal cause of this disease may be clearly traced to the abrupt change which took place in the dietary of the people, from potatoes and milk, and occasionally fish and meat, to the almost unvaried use of Indian meal, owing to the extravagant prices of the other farinaceous articles of food (flour, oatmeal, etc.) and to the scarcity of milk, from the fatality amongst cattle during the winter. That Indian meal is a nutritious article of food, is undeniable (particularly well fitted for those at active labour) but it is equally undeniable that it was the cause of much suffering and sickness, which may in a great degree be ascribed to its improper preparation, the grain being very coarsely ground, with the bran generally unseparated (which is far more irritating than the bran of wheaten flour), and the meal thus obtained used either boiled in water or made into hard, flat cakes, in either mode alike indigestible.

The distribution of food from the Relief Committee, in the shape of porridge (made of various kinds of meal boiled in water, with salt, spices and a faint trace of salt meat) also helped to produce and keep up dysentery.

The actual change of diet must also be considered as a powerful cause, for in previous years the supply of potatoes generally fell short, in most parts of Ireland, during June and July, when oatmeal became the ordinary article of diet among the poor, at which time every dispensary physician in the country districts had an unusual amount of cases of gastric affections applying for treatment. These causes combined, the change to a diet of indigestible, badly-cooked food, insufficient in quantity, with a general state of mental and physical depression, may be considered as the origin of dysentery.

In order to study its nature and symptoms with more accuracy and satisfaction, three sub-divisions or groups may be distinguished and called, 1st, the acute dysentery; 2nd, the ordinary form as it attacked adults; and 3rd, as it appeared in children; this division not being merely artificial, but the natural arrangement which suggested itself to my mind at the time and which was constantly acted upon in practice.

1 The symptoms of the first group generally came on suddenly, preceded by constipation for a few days, with excruciating pains all over the abdomen; expression of intense anguish and anxiety on the countenance, with rapid exhaustion; and general symptoms of the most severe kind. Its progress was very rapid, and frequently towards a fatal termination.

The medicines used in this variety were *Nux vomica* and *Mercurius*, which were generally administered in the commencement in frequently-repeated doses (half-hour or hour), either singly or in alternation, preceded or not by *Aconite,* according to the urgency and rapidity of the case. In the most urgent cases, *Arsenicum* and *Veratrum* were used with marked success where *Nux vomica* and *Mercurius* had been tried for a short time with little relief.

2 The ordinary form of dysentery, as it attacked adults, generally commenced with loss of appetite, nausea, and looseness of the bowels, which gradually increased, till in the course of four or five more days all the urgent symptoms of dysentery became developed.

It was in this class of cases that the effects of *Mercurius corrosivus* and *Nux vomica* were best seen, given singly, in succession, or alternately (according to each particular case), at intervals varying from two to six or eight hours. It was seldom found necessary to give *Aconite*, as the condition of the patient was rather the reverse of inflammatory, as indicated by slow and weak pulse, loss of strength, etc. *Arsenicum* or *Veratrum, Rhus* and *China* were also used in particular instances.

Anasarca in the limbs or trunk occasionally accompanied and followed dysentery in adults, and continued for some weeks after the healthy action in the intestines had been restored. The remedies used in it were almost the same as those previously described in the treatment of dropsy following fever.

3 Dysentery, as it appeared in children from the ages of one year to twelve or fourteen, differed in many respects from the same disease in adults, being more difficult of cure, and the symptoms peculiarly characteristic and more severe. Some of the principal points of difference were in the character of pain, in the enormous increase in development of the abdomen, the voracious appetite, the extreme degree of emaciation which ensued in most cases, the rare occurrence of anasarca, the higher ratio of mortality, and the predominance of symptoms at night.

The medicines found most useful in this class of cases were *Arsenicum, Veratrum, Nux vomica, Mercurius, Rhus tox., Sulphur, China, Secale.*

Towards the middle of June, the treatment of nearly two hundred cases having terminated, it was considered proper to bring my labours at Bantry to a close, sufficient time having elapsed to afford the system a full and complete trial, the amount of disease in the place also becoming rapidly diminished, and a new mode of relief being established, the erection of sheds for those suffering from fever and dysentery, with additional medical attendance, etc., under the provision of the new Poor Relief Act, passed by Parliament a short time previously.

The duration of my stay in Bantry extended from the 9th of April to 15th June, a period of 67 days, or nearly ten weeks, during which the total number of cases treated was:

	Fever[26]	111
	Dysentery[27]	<u>81</u>
		192
Fever:	Cases cured	108
	Dismissed	1
	Died	<u>2</u>
		111
Dysentery:	Cases cured	59
	Much improved	9
	Dismissed	2
	Died	<u>11</u>
		81

These results show a mortality of 1.8 % in fever and of 14% in dysentery.

These cases were all taken indiscriminately, as with the most perfect truth it can be said that no case was refused by me that came within a reasonable distance of my usual rounds, and that was without other medical attendance, regardless even of the most desperate cases, many of which were undertaken without a shadow of hope,[28] in accordance with my fixed determination to take all cases, without reserve or selection.

The particulars of each of the cases, with the names at full length, the time and duration of the disease, are printed in the Appendix.

The results above quoted consist of a series of reports drawn out from time to time for the committee of the Association, and ultimately completed to stand by themselves, in ignorance at that time of the results of the

---

[26] Twenty-four being cases of typhus, and eighty-seven continued fever

[27] Of these eighty-one patients, forty-eight were from the ages of 1 to 16 years; twenty-three from 16 to 50; and ten from 50 to 70. Of the forty-eight young persons, 4 died; of the twenty-three adults, 3; and of the ten old people, 4; which shows the mortality to have been by far the highest amongst old people.

[28] A glance at the reports of some of the fatal cases of dysentery in the Appendix will illustrate this statement.

treatment of the same diseases in the Bantry Union Hospital, which at my request were afterwards kindly forwarded to me by Doctor Tuckey, its physician, who copied the following table from the books. (see illustration)

Owing to the confusion consequent upon the illness of one of the physicians of the hospital, the results for April could not be obtained, so that we can only compare the results of homœopathic treatment during April, May, and the first half of June, with May, June and July of the Bantry hospital.

It is notorious that the months of April and May were the worst months of that year for fever, and March, April and May for dysentery, both in Bantry and all other parts of the county Cork (the mortality being then higher, and the amount greater). As we are thus precluded from a comparison with the results of precisely corresponding times, we are obliged to contrast our period, the greater part of which was at the worst time of those diseases with the period of the hospital results, the greater part of which corresponded with the improving time of the same diseases.

Even if we take this comparison as one on equal grounds, we find the total number of cases of dysentery admitted during those three months to have been 237, to which, adding 13, the difference between the number in the infirmary at the commencement, and the number at the close of the period, we have an aggregate of 250. Out of this aggregate, the deaths amount to 90, being a mortality of 36%, whilst the mortality under homœopathic treatment was only 14 per cent. Again, the number of completed cases of fever in that period in the hospital was 254; of these 35 died, showing a mortality of 13.8%; the mortality under homœopathic treatment being 1.8% in the same disease.

That those under homœopathic treatment, circumstanced as they were in general without proper food or drink, should have succeeded as well as the inmates of the hospital of the same town (taken precisely from the same class of people) with the advantages of proper ventilation, attendance, nourishment etc., would have been most gratifying; but that the rate of mortality under the homœopathic system should have been so decidedly in favour of our grand principle, is a circumstance, it may be hoped, which can scarcely fail to attract the attention even of the most sceptical.

We gladly avail ourselves of an opportunity of forming another very striking and interesting comparison on this subject.

An anonymous contributor in the number of the *Medico-Chirurgical Review* for April of this year, writing on this subject of the epidemic fever in Ireland and elsewhere, has given the following statistics of his own treatment of that disease, assisted by a colleague, in an hospital of which he had the chief management, which hospital is presumed, from his details, to have been in Liverpool or Manchester. It was established, he says, for the reception principally of emigrants from Ireland to this country during that spring and summer, and of others to whom the same epidemic fever had extended, as he shows, by contagion and contact with the Irish portion of the population.

Total number of cases of fever admitted into his hospital:

	Cases	Deaths	Proportion of Deaths
Under 15	686	59	1 in 11.66
15 – 30	1121	79	1 in 14.75
30 – 50	683	104	1 in 6.50
Above 50	172	45	1 in 3.66
	2662	287	1 in 9.66

A comparison of the rate of mortality in fever under homœopathic treatment, with those results, is very interesting, as being a complete answer to those who attempt to decry Homœopathy as a system of 'do-nothing expectant medicine.' This gentleman tells us that his treatment (custom?) was almost universally to abstain from all interference and to remain passively watching the cases, ordering them free ventilation, cleanliness and confinement to bed; simple diluents, water, or milk and water, being given as drinks (having found, he says, a simple saline, given purely as a placebo' in a few cases, to do harm). But although he congratulates himself upon the success attendant upon thus allowing the cases to take their natural course, undisturbed by medicine, except where lesions of particular organs seemed to render it imperative, we are compelled when we look upon the rate of mortality – upwards of 10% – to acknowledge its great height when compared with that under homœopathic treatment.

Were Homœopathy a system of 'expectant medicine' it might have fared about as well as this gentleman's practice[29]; but the contrast between 10% and 1.75% affords another brilliant example that homœopathic treatment, not disturbing the natural process at work in the occult phenomena of disease, still exerts a distinct and specific curative action, thereby shortening its duration and increasing the prospects of recovery.

If additional proof be required, it may be found in the testimony of those who had most opportunity of judging of the efficacy of the treatment, namely the resident clergymen of both persuasions, and of the gentry of the county forming the Poor Relief Committee, who, having heard of my departure from Bantry, forwarded to me in London letters and vote of thanks. To myself, individually, the most gratifying circumstance connected with this Irish Mission is in the delightful assurance that the grateful remembrance of many of the poor sufferers still holds, and that, in the words of a correspondent intimately acquainted with the poor of that neighbourhood, writing many months afterwards from Bantry, they 'yet continue to bless the means and the instrument which proved so useful to them in the time of their melancholy need and suffering.'

---

[29] The mortality under his mode of practice was actually less than that in the Bantry Hospital (as 10% – 14%) where the ordinary remedies of the old school were employed. Hence the plain inference that those remedies are positively injurious and should not be used; which inference extends far beyond fever, for the same result followed from a comparison of the rate of mortality in various acute diseases treated in Vienna by Dr Skoda, Physician of the General Hospital (Allopathic) in that city (by giving hay water as a 'placebo' and allowing the disease to follow its natural course) with the mortality under the ordinary remedies of the old school by his colleagues in the same hospital and with the results of homœopathic treatment in the same diseases by Dr Fleischmann, of the Vienna Homœopathic Hospital, in which comparison the mortality under the 'expectant system' was less than under the old school remedies, but greater than under homœopathic treatment.

APPENDIX.

IRISH MISSION.

Report from Mr. Kidd of Cases treated at Bantry, in Ireland, from the 9th of April to 15th of June, 1847.

Name.	Age.	Period & Nature of Disease	Duration of Treatment.		Result.
			Date.	No. of Days	
William Willis	19	2nd day of fever	April 9 to 13....	5	.... a
Margaret Rodgers	8	2nd do.	,, 12 to 21....	10	Cured.
Anne Harrington	8	14th do.	,, 12 to 21....	10	do.
Mary Hutchinson	34	3rd do.	,, 12 to 22....	11	do.
Mary Holland	27	4th do.	,, 15 to 23....	9	do.
John Collins	15	7th do.	,, 14 to 22....	9	do.
Jerry Sullivan	16	14th do.	,, 14 to 21....	8	do. } b
Thaddeus Sullivan	10	16th do.	,, 14 to 21....	8	do.
Ellen Sullivan	10	10th do.	,, 15 to 22....	8	do.
Mary Rogers	40	3rd do.	,, 12 to May 3	22	do.
Dolly Roohan	43	3rd do.	,, 12 to 26....	15	do.
Daniel Murphy	12	2nd do.	,, 22 to May 3	12	do.
Pat. Downey	34	10th do.	,, 13 to 26....	14	do.
Joseph Leary	30	5th do.	,, 13 to 30....	18	do.
Mary Sullivan	33	5th do.	,, 12 to 26..	15	do.
Jerry Sullivan	5	2nd do.	,, 22 to 27....	6	do.
John Downey	18	2nd day relapse of fever..	,, 18 to May 1	14	do.
Kate Regan	39	5th day of fever	,, 21 to ,, 1	11	do.
Con Carty	14	5th do.	,, 23 to ,, 3	11	do.
Pat. Sullivan	28	3rd do.	,, 23 to ,, 3	11	do.
Pat. Flynn	40	14th day relapse of fever.	,, 23 to 30....	8	do.
Dennis Flynn	16	12th day of fever	,, 15 to 29....	15	do.
John Downey	32	7th do.	,, 23 to 30....	8	do.
Mary Rogers	18	3rd do.	,, 28 to May11	14	do.
Johanna Sullivan	56	14th do.	,, 17 to ,, 7	21	do.
Mary Cronin	16	6th do.	,, 27 to ,, 8	12	do.
Mary Creemeen	50	8th do.	,, 14 to ,, 2	19	do. }
Kitty Creemeen	16	6th do.	,, 14 to ,, 2	19	do. } c
Pat. Creemeen	15	6th do.	,, 14 to ,, 2	19	do. }
Francis M'Evoy	13	7th do.	,, 17 to ,, 4	18	do.d
John Downey	32	7th do.	,, 23 to ,, 1	9	do.
Margaret Patterson	30	2nd do.	,, 28 to ,, 10	13	do.e
Tim. Cronin	24	12th do.	,, 27 to ,, 10	14	do.
Mary Harrington	30	2nd do.	,, 29 to ,, 10	12	do.
Johanna Collins	16	4th do.	,, 21 to ,, 10	20	do.
Patrick Nagle	35	3rd do.	,, 16 to 24....	9	do.f
Mary Hutchinson	34	12th do.	,, 16 to May 3	18	Died.g
Roger Humphrey	16	2nd do.	May 1 to 16 ...	16	Cured.
Richard Hutchinson	35	3rd do.	April28 to May14	17	do.h
Con Roohan	10	2nd do.	,, 24 to ,, 10	17	do.i

a Treatment discontinued, owing to disobedience to directions.

b These two were brothers, six of whose family were seized with fever about the same time. The day of my first visit, the father and one son were buried; and the week before, the mother and daughter died. Of the two survivors, I did not expect the youngest would live another day, and both were so far advanced in fever, that the prognosis was most unfavourable, in addition to which they were reduced to the lowest degree of depression by mental suffering, caused by the loss of the rest of their family and by their great destitution; notwithstanding these circumstances, however, they both recovered.

c These three lay on the same bed in very bad typhus, so bad that they were almost abandoned to their fate by their relatives.

d A case of cerebral typhus.

e A case of low typhoid fever in a phthisical subject.

f Relapsed on April 26th; was again under treatment to May 6th. Cured.

g She was almost convalescent April 26th; on the 28th, relapse ensued, with pleuritis, which proved fatal.

h Was almost convalescent May 6th, when a sad accident occurred to him. During a dreadful night's rain, he lay actually flooded in his bed from the rain pouring in on him from a chasm in the thatch of his cabin. He was so very weak as to be unable to move himself from the bed, and could derive no assistance from the rest of his family (4), who lay in fever at the other end of the wretched cabin, so that he was obliged to remain thus exposed for eight or ten hours till morning, when some charitable neighbour rescued him from the bed that had nearly proved a watery grave. As might have been expected, the fever returned more severely, and his convalescence proved tedious.

i Cured also of an attack of diarrhœa after the fever.

Dr. Kidd's Patients

Name.	Age.	Period & Nature of Disease	Duration of Treatment.		Result.
			Date.	No. of Days	
Judith Downey............	7	3rd day of fever	April 30 to May 7	8	Cured.
Mary Neal..................	14	12th day relapse of fever..	May 8 to 14......	7	do.
Jerry Harrington	30	6th day of fever.............	,, 10 to 14......	5	do.
Kate Collins.................	16	7th do.	,, 1 to 8......	8	do.
Pat. Collins	28	3rd do.	,, 4 to 13......	10	do.
Mary Leary	13	5th do.	,, 1 to 8......	8	do.
Pat. Leary...................	12	2nd do.	,, 5 to 14......	10	do.
Mary Healy	8	2nd do.	April 28 to May 8	11	do. }
Norah Healy	34	3rd do.	,, 26 to ,, 12	17	do. } j
Joan Healy...................	12	6th do.	,, 28 to ,, 8	11	do. }
Edward Healy	13	3rd do.	,, 28 to ,, 17	20	do. }
Cornelius Sullivan	35	10th do.	,, 26 to ,, 4	9	do.
Pat. Flynn....................	40	14th day relapse of fever..	,, 23 to ,, 4	12	do. k
John Harrington	22	14th day of fever.............	,, 28 to ,, 12	15	do.
Dan. Harrington	21	21st do.	,, 28 to ,, 8	11	do.
Kate Harrington	45	4th do.	May 1 to 12.......	12	do.
Judy M'Carthy	46	2nd wk. edema after fever	April 24 to 30	7	do.
Pat. O'Brien	35	2nd d. fever wh. pleuritis	May 6 to 24	19	do.
Daniel O'Brien..............	29	2nd day of fever.............	,, 7 to 22	16	do.
Pat. M'Carthy	46	7th do.	,, 12 to 21	10	do.
Rebecca Willis	23	3rd do.	,, 6 to 19	14	do.
Florence Rogers...........	13	2nd do.	,, 11 to 19	9	do.
Callaghan M'Carthy	21	5th do.	,, 10 to 26	17	do. l
Fanny Hutchinson	22	2nd do.	,, 4 to 20	17	do.
Susan Hutchinson	60	2nd do.	,, 6 to 21	16	do.
Jerry Rohan	48	3rd do.	,, 6 to 21	16	do.
Mary Hussey	34	6th do.	,, 10 to 24	15	do.
Cornelius Cotter...........	42	12th do.	,, 14 to 24	11	do.
Ellen M'Carthy	16	3rd do.	,, 16 to 25	10	do.
John Kiely...................	10	4th do.	,, 17 to 24	8	do.
Eugene M'Carthy	12	14th do.	,, 1 to 6	6	do.
Widow Downey..............	35	5th do.	,, 21 to 29	9	do.
Ellen Connolly	2	4th do.	,, 18 to 24	7	do.
John Connolly	35	4th do.	,, 17 to 24	8	do. m
Jerry Leary	14	3rd do.	,, 17 to 29	13	do.
Mary Driscoll................	5	3rd do.	,, 16 to 24	9	do.
Jerry Driscoll................	40	8th do.	,, 16 to 29	14	do. n
John Ford	30	6th do.	,, 14 to 28	15	do.
Norry Ford	23	2nd do.	,, 16 to 26	11	do. o
George Sullivan	21	3rd do.	,, 14 to 24	11	do.
Mary Sullivan	10	2nd do.	,, 21 to 26	6	do.
Widow Shea..................	45	3rd do.	,, 15 to 24	10	do.
Mary Sullivan	60	3rd do.	,, 21 to 28	8	do.
John Mahony	36	3rd do.	,, 22 to 28	7	do.
Pat. Mahony	12	4th do.	,, 23 to 28	6	do.
Pat. Harrington	4	2nd do.	,, 20 to 26	7	do.
Cornelius Regan	5	5th do.	,, 15 to 25	11	do.
Joseph Regan................	14	3rd do.	,, 11 to 30	20	do.
John Regan	19	1st do.	,, 11 to 24	14	do.
Mary Connor	5	6th do.	,, 8 to 16	9	do.
Pat. Hussey..................	32	6th day of fever, with pleuro-pneumonia	,, 10 to 18	9	Died. p
John Leary	18	3rd day of fever.............	,, 19 to June 1...	14	Cured.
Judith Cronin................	22	3rd do.	,, 21 to ,, 3..	14	do.
Kate Cronin.................	12	5th do.	,, 21 to ,, 9..	20	do.
Ellen Downey................	21	4th do.	,, 14 to 21	8	do. q.
Kate Downey.................	68	2nd do.	,, 23 to June 3..	12	do. r.
Johanna Sullivan	28	6th do.	,, 24 to ,, 2..	10	do.

j These four patients were members of the same family, the entire of whom I had under my care, and all (7) with favourable results.

k Relapsed again on May 7th, under treatment from that day to May 15th. Cured.

l This was a case of cerebral typhus attended for several days with furious delirium.

m This case was complicated with pleuritis.

n This was a most melancholy case of utter destitution, with his entire family (4) in fever, without straw to lie upon or clothes to cover him, without food, drink, or fire, till I directed the attention of the Rev. Mr. Hallowell to his case. After his convalescence, he was confined to bed (the earth floor) for a fortnight, for want of clothes to dress himself with.

o A case of low typhus, occurring soon after her accouchement.

p Along with the pulmonic complication, this person had to contend with extreme mental and physical depression, the effect of his sad destitution.

q Relapsed on May 24th, and was again under my care to June 2nd. Cured.

r This old woman was the fifth of one family under my care, all of whom recovered.

246   IRISH MISSION.

Name.	Age.	Period & Nature of Disease	Duration of Treatment.			Result.
			Date.	No. of Days		
John Cronin...................	22	5th day of fever..............	May 26 to June 2	8		Cured.
Giles Harrington............	40	2nd do.	,, 28 to ,, 7	11		do.
Margaret Ford..............	32	6th do.	,, 19 to ,, 5	18		do.ˢ
Daniel Sullivan..............	32	2nd do.	,, 27 to ,, 14	19		do.
Patrick Butler................	12	2nd do.	June 3 to 10	8		do.
Mary Butler..................	40	5th do.	May 23 to June 15	24		do.ᵗ
Mary Connor.................	36	2nd do.	,, 27 to ,, 2	7		do.
Dennis Harrington	35	1st do.	,, 26 to ,, 10	16		do.
John Harrington	3	1st do.	,, 27 to ,, 4	9		do.
Mary Carty..................	12	5th do.	,, 24 to ,, 2	10		do.
Mary Carty..................	45	5th do.	,, 26 to ,, 10	16		do.
Peggy Carty	6	3rd do.	,, 24 to ,, 2	10		do. ᵘ
John Carty	26	3rd do.	,, 24 to ,, 3	11		do.
Dennis Carty	21	2nd do.	,, 25 to ,, 2	9		do.

ˢ Relapsed on June 7th, was again under treatment to June 14th. Cured.
ᵗ A case of low typhus, with extreme nervous depression.
ᵘ Six members of this family recovered from fever under my care. Dennis Carty relapsed on June 4th, was again under my treatment to June 10th. Cured.

In the above statements, the date of recovery is fixed from the day on which the patient was so far well after the fever as not to require medicine, or where the patient was able to leave the bed with safety.

In most of the cases where relapse occurred, it was clearly traceable to the use of improper food, which the poor convalescent was frequently obliged to partake of, from the difficulty of obtaining a more digestible or wholesome description than Indian meal made into thick porridge or hard cakes. Rice was found to agree with the convalescents very well, but in many cases the supply of it was so small, that the weekly allowance was used in three or four days.

The drinks generally used by the fever patients were rice water, milk and water, cold water, and in a few cases whey.

The ages of the patients stated in the above and in the following report were ascertained as accurately as possible, but cannot be considered as absolutely exact.

It was an invariable rule to visit the patients occasionally, for at least a week after the treatment was discontinued, in order to ascertain if relapse should have occurred.

Name.	Age.	Period and Nature of Disease.	Duration of Treatment.		Result.
			Date.	No. of Days.	
Anne O'Connell	18	10th day of dysentery	April 11 to 19....	9	Cured.
Roger Donoghue....	2	7th day ditto	,, 17 to 22 ...	6	do.
Judith Sullivan	12	2nd week ditto	,, 15 to 22....	8	do.
Dan. Sullivan	54	7th day ditto	,, 13 to 16....	4	do.
Edward Healy......	60	8th week ditto	,, 13 to 19....	7	do.
Cornelius Healy....	35	4th day ditto	,, 15 to 21.. .	7	do.
James Butler	12	3rd day ditto	,, 15 to 22....	8	do.a
Dan. Hoolahan	15	3rd week ditto	,, 17 to 24....	8	do.
Mary Connor	2	6th week ditto	,, 14	1	Died.b
Tim. Harrington ...	6	3rd month ditto	,, 12 to 25....	14	Cured.
Dennis Harrington .	3	6th day ditto, with prolapsus ani................	,, 12 to 25....	14	do.
Eliza Hutchinson .	4	6th week ditto, with prolapsus ani................	,, 12 to 26 ...	15	do.
Thady Downey	6	6th week of dysentery	,, 13 to 28....	16	do.
Dennis Downey	7	2nd week ditto	,, 26 to May 3	8	do.
Michael Downey....	3	3rd month ditto	,, 12 to 30....	19	do.
Sally Harrington ..	28	4th week ditto, with general dropsy................	,, 15 to 21....	7	Died.c
Pat. Neal ,........	60	2nd week of dysentery	,, 13 to 30....	18	Cured.
Widow Shea........	50	4th month ditto	,, 15 to 24 ...	10	do.
Anne Holland	2	3rd day ditto	,, 17 to 26....	10	do.
Bridget Collins	24	7th week ditto	,, 22 to 28....	7	do.
Kitty Hickey	13	10th day ditto	,, 22 to 29....	8	do.
Sally Sullivan......	3	8th day ditto	,, 24 to 29....	6	do.
Kitty Healy	10	3rd wk. of diarrhœa aft. fever	,, 18 to 26...	9	do d
Thady Daly	13	5th day of dysentery........	,, 19 to May 1	13	do.
Jerry Foley	70	14th day ditto	,, 17 to 21....	5	Died. } e
Bridget Shinahan ..	70	6th month ditto	,, 14 to 19....	5	Died. }
John Holland	6	14th day ditto	,, 22 to 26....	5	do.
Anne Holland	2	3rd day ditto	,, 21 to 26....	6	do.
Mary Harrington....	6	6th week ditto	,, 15 to 18....	4	Died.
Johanna Downey ...	6½	3rd month ditto	,, 17 to May 3	17	Cured.f
Cornelius Holland..	35	8th day ditto	,, 13 to ,, 3	21	do.
Jer. Mahony	40	7th day ditto	,, 29 to ,, 10	12	do.g
Mary Crowley	24	6th wk of diarrhœa aft. fever	,, 29 to ,, 10	12	do.
Ellen Daly	10	5th week of dysentery, with prolapsus ani and extreme emaciation	,, 16 to 18...	2	Died.h
John Regan....	44	6th day of dysentery........	,, 14 to 19....	6	i
Tim. Donovan......	55	4th week ditto	,, 16 to 20....	5	Died.j
Fanny Cotter	21	4th wk. of diarrhœa aft. fever	,, 29 to May 10	12	Cured.
Patrick Daly	36	5th day of dysentery........	,, 19 to ,, 4	16	do.
Mary Daly	9	14th day ditto	,, 19 to ,, 4	16	do.
Mary Sullivan......	3	2nd week ditto	,, 23 to ,, 8	16	do.
Mary Daly	14	6th week ditto	,, 16 to 24....	9	do.k
Murphy Shea	50	4th day ditto	May 1 to 6	6	do.

a This case was attended for some days with violent inflammatory fever.
b This child was a most frightful spectacle of emaciation through disease and starvation. She died in twelve hours after my first visit.
c This was a most wretched case. Having lost all her family by disease, in the country, near Bantry, she crawled into the town and lay for two or three weeks in a corner of a cabin, about ten feet square, and without a window, depending on the charity of those about her, almost as poor as herself. In the room where she lay there were four persons huddled together, part in fever and the rest in dysentery.
d Diarrhœa after fever was a most formidable disease amongst convalescents, and caused more deaths than even the original fever.
e The mortality amongst very old people during the epidemic was most enormous, recovery being rather the exception to the general rule, which, however, never prevented me from undertaking such. Several recoveries in very old people from fever and dysentery, may be seen in the reports.
f This case was attended with dropsy.
g This case was attended for four or five days with violent inflammatory fever.
h In this case the treatment could not have had a fair opportunity in two days.
i Treatment discontinued for disobedience of directions, &c.
j This case was reported (and with justice) in the town as being a death by actual starvation.
k After a lapse of five or six days she was again attacked by the dysentery, which proved fatal in six hours.

Name.	Age.	Period and Nature of Disease.	Duration of Treatment.		Result.
			Date.	No. of Days.	
Tim. Burke	6	4th month of dysentery, with extreme emaciation and prolapsus ani	April 19 to 27	9	Died.l
Judy M'Carthy	12	3rd day of dysentery........	May 10 to 17	8	Cured.
John Hussey	6	2nd week ditto	April 28 to May 8.	11	do.
Kitty M'Carthy	40	3rd week ditto	,, 28 to ,, 13	16	do.
Dennis Collins......	16	7th day ditto	,, 24 to 27....	3	Died.m
Mary Leary	15	3rd wk. of diarrhœa aft. fever	May 10 to 17	8	Cured.n
Nugent Sullivan	7	14th day of dysentery, with prolapsus ani	April 15 to May 13	29	do.
Norry Downey......	40	1st day of dysentery, followed by ileus..................	,, 16 to ,, 1	16	Died o
John Donovan......	42	4th day of dysentery....... .	,, 30 to ,, 12	13	Cured.
Ellen M'Namara....	32	6th day ditto	,, 28 to ,, 16	19	do.
John Mahoney......	4	3rd week ditto	,, 28 to ,, 12	15	do.
Kate Mahoney......	8	3rd week ditto	,, 28 to ,, 12	15	do.
Pat. Hickey	8	4th week ditto	,, 22 to ,, 6	15	......p
Jerry Roohan	4	3rd day ditto	May 12 to 17	6	Cured.
Dennis Harrington..	4	2nd week ditto	,, 20 to 28	9	do.
John Sullivan	4	2nd week ditto .... ,	,, 12 to 20	9	do.
Mary Minahan......	4	3rd week ditto	April 17 to May 5	19	Much imp.
Con Minahan	5	2nd week ditto	,, 21 to ,, 10	20	do.
Mary Neal..........	7	8th week ditto	,, 28 to ,, 12	15	Cured.q
Kitty Casey	18	6th wk. of diarrhœa aft. fever	May 8 to 31	24	do.
Catherine Shehan ..	3	2nd week of dysentery	,, 15 to 23 ..	9	do.
James Shehan......	1	3rd week ditto	,, 20 to 31 ..	12	do.
Edmund Barry	48	6th day ditto	,, 12 to 27 ..	16	do.
John Baker	5	2nd week ditto	,, 1 to 14	14	do.
Kitty Burke........	4	7th week of dysentery, with prolapsus ani	,, 1 to 14	14	do.
Kate Leary	64	7th day of dysentery........	,, 28 to June 5	9	do.r
Kate M'Carthy	4	6th week ditto, with prolapsus ani	,, 1 to 14	14	Much imp.
Judy M'Carthy	2	10th day of dysentery........	,, 1 to 16	16	Cured.
Michael Harrington.	22	3rd week ditto	,, 6 to June 10	36	Much imp.
James Harrington..	20	7th day ditto	,, 6 to ,, 10	36	do.s
Mary Hickey	17	4th day ditto	,, 18 to ,, 5	19	Nearly well.t
John Kennedy......	18	7th day ditto	,, 1 to ,, 10	41	Cured.
Horace Minahan....	4	8th day of diarrhœa aft. fever	,, 12 to ,, 8	27	Nearly well.u
Mary Minahan	21	6th day of dysentery........	,, 13 to ,, 4	22	Cured.
Tim. M'Carthy.....	50	10th day ditto	,, 8 to 29	22	Died.v
Mary M'Carthy	32	6th day ditto ,........	,, 25 to June 6	12	Cured.w
Catherine Carty	7	4th week ditto	,, 18 to ,, 3	16	do.
John Carty	3	10th day ditto	,, 16 to ,, 9	24	Much imp.
Dennis Hoolahan....	5	2nd week ditto	,, 24 to ,, 10	17	do.x

l The last of seven brothers, who all died of dysentery in a few months.

m Of all my sad experience in dysentery, this case was the most severe and the most rapid in its progress.

n This case was complicated with prolapsus ani.

o She was convalescent and out of bed for four or five days, when a sudden return of the disease proved fatal in eight hours (during my absence from Bantry).

p Treatment discontinued on account of the unavoidable use of improper food.

q This case was attended with severe inflammatory fever for several days.

r This old woman was very feeble and reduced by want of sufficient or proper food.

s In these two cases the disease was kept up for a long time by the use of improper food.

t In this case, distortion of the bones took place from want of muscular support, owing to her long continued want of food, causing emaciation. She was the child of a mendicant.

u This was a very severe case and attended with prolapsus ani.

v This poor man had been almost starved in the country, and as a last resource took refuge in the town, when his strength was almost gone, and he was therefore unable to work.

w The wife of the last patient.

x This boy was deaf and dumb.

15, George St., Hanover Sq.: Tuesday, Thursday, Saturday, 10 to 2.
1, Finsbury Circus, City: Monday, Wednesday, Friday, 10 to 2.
No appointments made; no one seen at any particular hour. Patients are received as nearly as possible in the order of arrival.

Those who arrive late, incur the risk of being too late, finding perhaps fifteen or twenty before them; enough to fill up the day.

The attendant has only one rule to follow—to send in the patient longest in the house. At one o'clock a fresh list is made. Those actually in the house are put first. They who arrive after one, no matter how early their names have been entered, are put at the bottom.

Under any circumstances please do not return after two o'clock, as to do so causes much trouble and inconvenience.

Dr. Kidd's waiting room chart

5   ON THE FEVER AND DYSENTERY OF IRELAND IN 1847

READ BEFORE THE BRITISH HOMŒOPATHIC SOCIETY ON THURSDAY, DECEMBER 2ND, BY MR. KIDD, SURGEON, MEMBER OF THE BRITISH HOMŒOPATHIC SOCIETY.

Mr. President and Gentlemen,

The following remarks on Fever and Dysentery are the result of my observations of the late Epidemic in Ireland, from the first week of April to the second week of June of the present year, whither I went, at the request of the Committee of the English Homœopathic Association, for the purpose of assisting in the relief of that trying period, by extending the advantages of Homœopathic treatment to a portion of the sufferers. The place which I selected for my residence was Bantry, a small town with a population of about 5,000 in the West of the County of Cork, situated near the bay of that name, in the midst of a poor, ill-cultivated country and within a few miles of those places immortalised in the annals of suffering and distress – Skibbereen and Skull. The reasons which induced me to select it as the sphere of operations were, first, that the amount of distress and disease exist-ing there at the time was very great; indeed it was represented to me by those most conversant with the state of that country (some of the resident gentry) as exceeding the condition of any part of the County Cork; and second, that the amount of ordinary medical attendance there was totally insufficient for the amount of disease, owing to the illness of one of the principal physicians and to the increase of sickness.

My patients belonged to the very poorest class, and were not able to obtain even the chance visits of the Dispensary Physician, who even at such a time refused to attend them, except on the usual recommendation of a sub-scriber, which was completely beyond the reach of the greater part of the wretched sufferers, whose condition it is painful to think of, crowded into small ill-ventilated huts with most insufficient clothing, and a scanty portion (bordering on actual starvation) of unwholesome, badly cooked food and in the lowest state of mental depression from the effects of their pitiable destitution; whilst the healthy remained in the closest contact with the diseased, and in many cases, Fever and Dysentery on the same bed of suffering.

Considering these circumstances, and the immense amount of actual physical labour required to visit each from house to house, frequently at considerable distances apart, and to remain for hours exposed to the pestilential miasmata of Fever and Dysentery in hovels crowded with human beings in the most loathsome state of uncleanliness, you can get a faint idea of the difficulties to be overcome in my enterprise, the success of which you can form your own estimate of after hearing the
following details.

FEVER
The history of fever as it appeared in Ireland last season, is very interesting in a medical point of view, from the intimate connexion which it has proved to exist between Famine and Fever, as cause and effect; for the spread of the former with very few deviations marked out the progress of the latter, and where most distress and destitution prevailed, there was most Fever to be found, and in general with most severity; however, as far as my observations extended, the actual amount of Fever was in a much more constant ratio to the extent of Famine, than was the type or character, which varied very much in different localities.

A few remarks on the subject of the distress will be found necessary, in order to elucidate more clearly the history of the Fever. The amount of destitution existing in Bantry and its neighbourhood was very great, and although not brought so prominently before the public as the condition of those places so near it (Skibbereen and Skull) where the attention of Government and the public was early called to their state by the active exertions of some of their resident gentry; still, from all I have heard and seen, I should feel inclined to say that Bantry and its neighbourhood suffered even more severely than those places, owing to the want of that active interference on the part of the resident gentry in which those who ought to have

77

been most active, and on whom most responsibility rested, were found most wanting, both as to personal exertions and pecuniary assistance. One glance at the crowd daily surrounding the soup kitchen in the town would have sufficed to tell a sad story; half-naked and emaciated forms with starvation depicted on their wild and haggard faces, where every process of bone stood out in relief, looking as if dirty parchment was drawn tightly over the skeleton, waiting with impatience for the moment of serving out their scanty pittance (about twenty ounces of porridge, containing four or five ounces of solid nutriment, at first without any bread, but at a later period with four ounces of biscuit) which to most constituted their sole support (if support that could be called which was a mere dragging out of existence, midst misery and want) for on the most creditable evidence it was known that most of those waiting till perhaps six or eight o'clock in the evening for its distribution had not tasted food since the corresponding hour the day previously; and the finding of persons dead by the road sides became so frequent an occurrence that it almost failed to attract notice in the country, or to cause a coroner's inquest to be considered necessary.

As might be expected from such a state of distress, Fever and Dysentery increased to a most frightful extent, so much so, that in April it was calculated by the Clergymen and myself, from an actual inspection of the greater part of the town, that upwards of 400 persons, or nearly one tenth of the entire population, were confined by these diseases; and the mortality in the town became so large that it was found necessary to have coffins constructed with sliding bottoms and to have horses and men employed by the Relief Committee to bury the dead, whose surviving relatives could seldom provide decent interment or even accompany them to the grave.

The predisposing causes of Fever may be enumerated –

1st, Famine, the most important and active of all.
2nd The frequent changes of weather and the imperfect clothing to resist such influences.
3rd The utter absence of proper ventilation in their wretched houses, over-crowded with fresh occupants daily entering the town from the surrounding country.
4th The sad prostration of mental energy and the depression of spirits caused

by their increasing destitution, a feeling which acted most injuriously during the course of Fever and to counteract which was found most difficult.

The actual exciting cause of fever could in most cases be traced to contagion, acting frequently in the dense crowd surrounding the soup kitchen, where were congregated healthy and diseased; those who not yet half convalescent from Fever, were obliged to go themselves in search of food to avert actual starvation. The total impossibility of separating the infected from the healthy portion of a family, proved also a very fertile source of contagion.

An exciting cause almost peculiar to adult males was over-exertion attended by exposure to the weather, three-fourths of the adult male population being employed on the public roads, having to walk from three to five miles from their houses to the place of work in the morning and the same in the evening when the system would be least able to resist such influences as piercing winds and drenching showers acting on frames enfeebled by insufficient food and over-exertion. Many of these cases (adult males) were attended with active inflammation of the lungs or pleura, or of both.

The most prevailing type of Fever, was continued Fever or Synocha, generally attended by catarrhal and rheumatic symptoms or gastric disturbance. There was also a good deal of typhus, attended by extreme nervous depression and debility, and some cases of Inflammatory Typhus, with raving, furious delirium and other indications of cerebral implication.

The symptoms of Synocha generally set in after exposure to contagion or changes of weather, with dryness and heat of the skin, heaviness and dull aching pains over the frontal region and in the eyelids, or throbbing pain at the temples; tongue dry, covered with whitish, yellowish or brownish fur in the centre and slightly red around the edges; mouth dry and clammy with much thirst; no appetite; nausea and vomiting with soreness at Epigastrium; bowels costive; urine very little changed, generally rather deeper in colour than natural, without deposit and scanty; cough, either hard, dry and difficult or attended with thick whitish, yellowish or greenish expectoration and in many cases sharp pricking pains in the chest; or cough, with obstruction of breathing and scanty expectoration, or thick and tenacious, streaked with blood; pulse rapid, hard and bounding, but wanting volume; aching or shooting pains in the bones and joints of the extremities (mostly of the lower), aggravated by movement; with soreness and aching in the muscular part of the limbs, which were generally described as being dead and heavy, rendering the slightest motion impossible; restlessness and sleeplessness at night, with anxiety and tossing, sometimes with nocturnal delirium, often caused by harassing cough with little or no expectoration.

The medicines used were – *Aconite* in almost every case at the commencement of treatment, and for some days, as long as the skin continued dry and hot, and the pulse accelerated; as soon as the inflammatory action had been in some degree subdued by *Aconite, Bryonia* was given at intervals of from three to six hours, under the action of which the heaviness over the eyes and the aching in the limbs were much ameliorated, against which symptoms it proved a perfect specific, as they almost invariably remained till after its administration, when their removal quickly followed.

Bryonia was also found very useful in cases attended with symptoms of pleuritis or pleuro-pneumonia particularly whilst inflammatory action continued in the general indications (with an occasional dose of *Aconite)* in which cases also *Phosphorus* was found most useful either after or in alternation with *Bryonia* (Of the many cases attended with inflammation of the lungs and pleura, I did not observe one of pure pneumonia, uncomplicated with pleuritis). *Belladonna* was given to obviate the distressing sleeplessness and restlessness at night, or where much delirium existed, and also against hard dry cough at night preventing rest.

Nux vomica was found necessary in cases attended with gastric irritation, nausea, soreness at epigastrium, aggravated by taking food or drink or where the tongue continued dry and furred after all trace of feverish action had been subdued; it was selected because of those particular sufferings resulting from irritating vegetable food or from coffee; in most cases of relapse from fever it was also used (as explained under that article); and against particular bronchitic symptoms. *Rhus* was used where the joints (knees, shoulders etc.) were more affected than the bones or muscles of the extremities, particularly in the latter stages of Fever, where much debility existed. In a few of those cases it was found more useful in alternation with *Bryonia* than given alone. *China* and *Sulphur* were given where all inflammatory action had ceased, and where convalescence was tedious but without any striking result, the cause generally being the want of proper or the use of improper nourishment and therefore beyond the reach of all medicine.

To illustrate this class of Fever cases, the details of three are added.

CASE 1

M.H., aged thirty-four years, visited first on 12th April, the third day of fever. complains of severe aching pains in the bones and joints of the extremities, aggravated by movement; throbbing headache at forehead and temples; the pulse is full and frequent; skin dry and hot; tongue dry, covered with white fur; bowels costive; very little sleep at night; short, hacking cough in the morning, without expectoration.
Tinct. *Aconite*, 3 gtt. iij.
in twelve spoonfuls of water, one to be taken every two hours.

14th – The skin still dry and hot; bowels relieved; very restless at night.
Rept *Aconite*, a dose 3tiis. horis
Tinct. *Bell.*, 3, gtt, j, at night.

17th – Skin soft and cool; perspiring; tongue coated but moist; less restlessness at night.
    Much cough in the morning, with scanty thick white expectoration.
Tinct. *Nux vomica*, 3, gtt, ij, 1/10 4tis. horis

19th – Scarcely a trace of fever; the cough is better and expectoration increased; sleeps well. To continue.
22nd – She is up and feels pretty strong; a little cough during the day.

24th – From exposure to cold draughts of air she has suffered a relapse; complains today of aching pains in the limbs; much cough with thick yellow

expectoration; pulse rapid but weak; skin hot and moist.
Tinct. *Bryonia*, 3 gtt. iij, 1/12 3tiis. horis

26th – Much better; less aching in the limbs; skin cool and soft; cough continues the same.
Rept. *Bryonia*, 1/12 6tis. horis

28th – Improving, and to continue.
30th – She is again able to leave the bed.

CASE II
J.D., aged forty years; visited May 16th, eight day of fever; complains of aching pains in all the bones, with sense of deadness in the limbs and inability to move them.
Cold shivering fits at times; skin dry and hot; pulse frequent, very weak; heaviness and aching in the forehead; tongue dry and furred; constant cough, attended with sharp stitch-like darting pains in the left side of chest and thin, scanty expectoration. (He is very low spirited, lying on the earthen floor of a cold damp room, with scarcely a trace of covering and without food or drink.)
Tinct. *Aconite*, 3, gtt. iij, 1/20 omni hora.

18th – The symptoms very little changed.
Tinct. *Bryonia*, 3, gtt. iij, 1/20 2dis. horis.
21st – Pulse less frequent; skin cool and moist; the pains in bones and chest continue very severe.
Rept. *Bryonia*, 1/12 3tiis. horis.

24th – Cough is rather better; now attended with much oppression of breathing, thick yellow expectoration; no headache; less aching in limbs.
Tinct. *Phosphorus*, 3, gtt. ij, 1/12 3tiis. horis.

26th – Cough much better; very little trace of fever.
To continue taking the *Phos*.
28th – Nearly well. No medicine.

30th – He is convalescent.

CASE III

M.C., aged forty-five years; visited May 24th, the fifth day of fever; complains of general aching pains in the bones and soreness in the muscles, aggravated by movement; pulse is full and frequent; skin hot and moist; tongue covered with a whitish layer of paste-like substance; no sleep at night; general feeling of nervousness and anxiety.
Tinct. *Bryonia*, 3 gtt. iij, 1/12 3tiis. horis.

27th – The aching in bones still very severe, but less fever.
Rept. *Bryonia*

30th – Fever almost gone; skin is cool; pulse quiet; very little headache; she is very restless at night. To continue
June 2nd – Convalescent.

4th – From the use of improper food she has suffered a relapse; the tongue is densely coated with whitish fur, soft and tremulous; soreness at epigastrium, aggravated by food or drink; shooting pains in the temples; general feeling of restlessness and uneasiness with despair of recovery.
Tinct. *Nux vomica*, 3, gtt.2, 1/8 3tiis. horis

6th – Still very weak and excited; symptoms much the same.
To continue taking the *Nux vomica.*

8th – Tongue becoming clean and moist; less pain at
epigastrium. She is very restless at night, and has had very
little sleep for some nights.
Tinct. *Bell.*, 3, gtt. ij, 1/12 4tis. horis.

10th – She is almost well; slept soundly last night.
No medicine
12th – Convalescent.

The symptoms of typhus were in general, in the early stages, dryness and heat of skin, quickly becoming reduced to the natural standard (often far below that) and constantly damped by cold clammy perspiration; tongue dry and glazed, hard like leather, covered with brownish yellow fur, in a few cases of uniform dark red colour, like the lean of raw beef; gums and teeth covered with sordes; constant thirst; nausea, with sickness; abdominal symptoms in some cases; flatulence; tension and tympanitic resonance of the parietes; occasional tenderness upon pressure over the cæcum; bowels costive or relaxed with griping pain; urine very seldom abnormal; heaviness and aching in forehead, with vertigo and sense of emptiness in the head; constant delirium, with low muttering or heavy stupid insensibility, with incoherence of speech; dull inanimate lustreless appearance of eyes, with the head turned away from light; excessive prostration of strength; falling down to the bottom of the bed and picking at bedclothes; where consciousness existed, there were great mental depression and anxiety; restlessness and want of sleep at night to a most distressing extent; harassing cough at night, with thin white mucous expectoration; or thick and hard, choking up the bronchi (from the patient's inability to expel it), and thereby impeding respiration; sensation of deadness and inability to move the lower extremities (without the acute aching pain usually present in the former class of cases); feet and legs cold and damp.

The pulse varied much in different cases, in some being rapid, small and weak, in others slow, languid and feeble, often difficult to be felt.

There were also some cases of inflammatory typhus, with full, hard and frequent pulse; hot dry skin; furious delirium, raving, mania; redness and prominence of the eyes, with intolerance of light and contracted pupils; involuntary discharge of urine, etc.

The medicines used in typhus were *Aconite*, where treatment commenced early in the disease, or where heat and dryness of skin were prominent among the symptoms; however in most cases it was not found indicated at any period of the disease. *Bryonia* and *Rhus, Phosphorus* and *Arsenicum*, were the medicines most used. *Bryonia* where heavy, stupid headache in the frontal region existed, with aching and sense of deadness in the lower limbs; moist skin; foul tongue, covered with a thick layer of yellowish or brownish fur, or with a thick tenacious paste, like a layer of putty spread over the tongue; nausea; vomiting, with painful sensibility at the epigastrium (against those symptoms of tongue and stomach it was found most particularly serviceable); also when there were cough, with pleuritic stitches in the side, restlessness and anxiety.

Rhus was frequently given in those cases, either alone, or in alternation with *Bryonia*, particularly in the latter stage, where all inflammatory action had ceased, and when symptoms of debility quickly followed; with dull haziness of the eyes; listless expression of face; coldness of skin, covered with clammy perspiration; small weak pulse; increased anxiety and restlessness; loss of consciousness and low delirium.

Arsenicum, where utter prostration of strength appeared; the patient falling down to the bottom of bed, and lying flat and listless, unable to move or speak with dry, hard and glazed tongue, or covered with dark-brown sordes; thirst; nausea and vomiting; hiccough; colicky pains in abdomen, with frequent liquid evacuations; small wiry pulse, irregular or intermittent.

Phosphorus, where oppression at the chest and difficulty of breathing appeared, with pleuritic stitches in the chest, and harassing cough, with thick yellowish or reddish expectoration.

Belladonna, where the delirium was of an active character, with furious raving, restlessness and obstinate absence of sleep; redness and prominence of eyes, with intolerance of light; wild expression of features, with fullness and redness of face etc.

Nux vomica, towards the termination of the disease, when *Bryonia* was found insufficient to remove the dense coating of fur from the tongue, or the tenderness and pain at epigastrium.

CASE IV

J.D., age about forty years; visited May 19th, sixth day of typhus; the symptoms were slight heat and dryness of skin; vertigo and dizziness of the head, with pain in the forehead which he cannot describe; raving and incoherence of speech at times (addressing absent persons and miscalling those about him; then suddenly recollecting their faces); heaviness and insensibility during the day and low delirium at night; very little sleep; he lies for hours in a heavy insensible state, not actual sleep; tongue flaccid, soft and tremulous, covered with a dense layer of whitish-yellow paste, coming off in flakes, on being rubbed with the finger, shewing the surface of the tongue beneath to be pale bright red; constant thirst.

Cough at times, attended with difficulty of breathing, mostly at night, and scanty thin expectoration; pulse soft, weak and slow; sensation of deadness from the hips to the feet, with dull aching pain.
Tinct. *Aconite*, 3, gtt, ij, 1/12 omni hora.

May 20th – No change; he has been very restless all night and raving; also much cough, with scanty thin expectoration.
Tinct. *Bell.*, 3, gtt. ij, 1/8 3tiis. horis.

22nd – Slept pretty well last night; the stomach inclined to vomiting; tongue the same; he is very weak and low; cannot support himself for a moment in the sitting posture.
Tinct. *Bryonia* 3, gtt. iij, 1/15 2dis. horis

24th – Very little change in any of the symptoms.
Rept. *Bryonia*

27th – Much oppression about the chest; very little cough.
Tinct. *Phos.* 3, gtt. ij, 1/10 3tiis. horis.

30th – He is excessively weak; lies almost insensible at bottom of bed; low muttering at times.
Tinct. *Arsenicum*, 3, gtt. ij, 1/12 3tiis, horis

June 2nd – He now sleeps a good deal, night and day; the other symptoms very little changed.
Rept. *Ars.*

5th – No cough; less delirium; the tongue is even more densely coated with the same paste-like substance.
Tinct. *Nux-v.,* gtt. ij, 1/6 6tis. horis
7th – All the symptoms improving; the tongue is gradually clearing around the edges and consciousness returning.
To continue taking *Nux-v.*

9th – Becoming convalescent.

12th – All symptoms of fever are gone; his strength is returning but very slowly.

CASE V

K.D., an old woman upwards of seventy years of age; visited May 23rd, the second day of fever; slight heat of the skin, which is covered with a clammy perspiration; aching and heaviness in the forehead, with vertigo and sense of 'bewilderment;' tongue rough, dry, of a dark brown colour (looking like a piece of leather); mouth dry, constant thirst; very little sleep; pulse slow, small and weak; general lassitude and debility.

Tinct. *Bryonia,* 3 gtt. 2, 1/12 3tiis. horis.

25th – Much the same; she was very restless all night; no sleep.
Rept. *Bryonia,* to be taken during the day.
Tinct. *Bell.* gtt. j, in two doses to be taken in the evening.

28th – Improving: the tongue today is of a bright red colour (like a piece of raw meat) interspersed with patches of white.
Tinct. *Bell.* 3 gtt. j, 1/8 4tis. horis.

31st – Much improved: the tongue becoming soft and moist, pale at the edges; sleeps well; appetite returning. No medicine

June 3rd – She is convalescent.

CASE VI (INFLAMMATORY TYPHUS)

Fs Mc E., age thirteen years; visited April 17th, the seventh day: complains of aching pains in the limbs, most severe about the knees, aggravated by movement or pressure; shooting pains in the forehead and temples, with sense of weight and heaviness over the eyes; he is restless and raving at night; cannot sleep; pulse rapid, full and hard; skin burning hot and dry; tongue red along the edges, dry, brown and furred in the centre; *very little thirst;* bowels regular. There is a general appearance of debility; the eyes look dull and lustreless; absence of expression in the features; inability to remain sitting for a moment (the pulse indicates the reverse of debility).

Tinct. *Acon* 3, gtt. iij. 1/12 2dis. horis

18th – He has been raving furiously all night, starting up in bed and screaming, with wild looks.
Tinct. *Bell*. 3, gtt. iij, 1/10 omni hora.

19th – No change in the symptoms. Rept. *Bell*.

20th – Complains today of the extreme degree of severity of pain in the lower limbs and joints; screams if they be touched.
Tinct. *Bryonia*, 3, gtt. iij, 1/10 3tiis. horis

22nd – The delirium is becoming constant and more furious, with redness of the conjunctiva of the eyes; intolerance of light; he is cross, peevish and fretful; the skin continues obstinately dry and hot; pulse rapid and full.
Tinct. *Bell.*, 3, gtt. iij, 1/20 2dis horis
Tinct. *Aconite,* 3, gtt. j, every eighth hour.

23rd – No improvement in any of the symptoms. To continue taking the medicines as last prescribed.

25th – Copious perspiration has appeared *on the back*, the rest of the skin continuing dry; constant delirium all night, less furious, with low muttering and picking at the bedclothes; he is very cross; much difficulty in giving him medicine; he still screams if the knees be touched.
Tinct. *Bryonia,* 3, gtt. iij, 1/12 3tiis horis

27th – Improving; the skin becoming cool and moist; tongue still coated in centre, moist and pale at the edges; consciousness returning; he appears to be quite deaf in both ears.
Tinct. *Rhus,* 3, gtt. iij, 1/8 4tis horis.

28th – Copious perspiration all over the body; all the symptoms much relieved.
To continue taking *Rhus* every six hours.

29th – Slept well last night for the first time during his illness; the deafness is disappearing; at times he is heavy and stupid.
Rept. Rhus, 1/8 night and morning

May 1st – No trace of fever; the deafness is almost gone.
No medicine

4th – He is up and gaining strength.

The convalescence of the fever patients was most rapid; indeed too much so in the generality of cases of simple continued fever, for the poor sufferers, finding their strength to be so quickly restored, were very apt to make too free with the cold air and to partake largely of indigestible food (Indian meal cakes or porridge or even of rice) the result of which was that nearly one-sixth of all the cases of continued fever suffered relapse to a fever of a far worse character than the original; it generally occurred about the second or third day after all traces of the original fever had disappeared; and in most, the cause above assigned could be clearly traced, which the first glance at the symptoms immediately confirmed. In a few, exposure to cold or to draughts of air proved the exciting cause.

Every possible effort was made to guard against this disagreeable consequence by restraining the patients to the bed or to the room as long as a single symptom remained, and by giving careful directions as to diet and also by explaining the dangerous nature of the relapse fever; but in many cases (as might naturally be expected) without success.

Convalescents after fever generally feel a very sharp appetite for the first or second week after the cessation of that disease, to restrain which would require more philosophy and reasoning power than those wretched creatures could be supposed to have possessed, particularly at such a time, with the dread of actual starvation hanging over them and no food but the most distasteful and indigestible within their reach.

The food found to agree best with the convalescents was – rice, boiled in water or milk; in some cases white bread and milk, boiled or not; however those were obtainable in a comparatively small number of instances; where they were, and taken in moderation, relapse did not follow. Almost without an exception, every one of those cases were again taken under treatment and entered, NOT AS FRESH CASES, *but in the original* report of each (as in the description of cases I and III).

The symptoms of the relapse fever were, in general, throbbing, shooting pains in the forehead and vertex, with vertigo; flushing of face with expression of intense anxiety and restlessness; despair of recovery; eyes dull and inanimate; quivering of the eyelids, tongue presenting one almost unvarying character, being *soft, tremulous, moist,* densely loaded with white paste; nausea, sickness; vomiting, often to a most distressing extent, with soreness at epigastrium, aggravated by pressure, food or drink; bowels generally relaxed, with slight griping pain or constipated; skin burning hot and moist; pulse slightly accelerated, irregular and weak; constant agitation and restlessness, with loss of sleep.

Nux vomica (Tinct. 3) was found to be the most certain and most serviceable medicine in those cases (sometimes preceded by a few doses of *Aconite*); under its action the tongue becoming clean, skin cool and the headache disappearing; so that, in a few days (from about four to eight), the patient was again in a fair way towards recovery, but with an increased degree of weakness.

Bryonia was tried in some of such cases, but with very little of the success with which the use of *Nux vomica* was attended, except where a return of the aching or shooting pains in the limbs, or of the pectoral symptoms took place, with more or less of the gastric derangement, in which it again proved its vast utility.

Arsenicum album was given when much depression and debility ensued, with the gastric symptoms, after the previous employment of *Nux vomica.*

Two or three of those suffered a second relapse and were again treated with success.

Relapse followed typhus much less frequently, in proportion to the number of cases, than continued fever, which happy immunity was principally owing to the return of strength being more gradual, and the appetite not being so soon restored, which rendered the convalescents more careful in taking food and in going into the open air.

Where relapse did follow typhus, it approached more closely in character to the original fever than did the relapse of continued fever to its original type and, as might have been expected, with an increased degree of debility and exhaustion, which rendered it more dangerous and fatal than ordinary typhus; one of the two deaths from fever being in relapse after typhus (the second was in a case of continued fever, with pleuro-pneumonia).

As health became restored to the convalescents, and as they reverted to their old mode of diet, diarrhœa frequently followed, particularly after typhus, or where much debility had previously existed; it was most usual in old persons, or in young, from about the ages of six to sixteen years. From the utter impossibility of removing the exciting cause in most cases, it generally proved a tedious and distressing complaint; at one time being almost cured but again breaking out, as the cause came into more active operation; however, towards the latter part of my labours it seldom occurred, owing to a supply of rice obtained for the use of the convalescents from the British Association Relief Committee.

The symptoms were in general frequent, thin, yellowish, brownish evacuations, sometimes tinged with blood and at first attended with shooting pain across the abdomen and flatulence, but in the latter stages without pain; in children prolapsus ani and rapid emaciation, in whom the attendant voracious appetite, keeping up the irritation, rendered it more difficult of cure.

The medicines used were *Arsenicum album* in the commencement where much shooting pain existed, with rapid appearance of debility and femaciation.

Rhus, China, Secale, etc. were given in the latter stage, where frequent pale evacuations, without pain and with increasing debility, were the most prominent symptoms; where the motions were bloody, with tenesmus, prolapsus ani, *Nux vomica* and *Mercurius corrosivus* were found necessary.

These, with as much attention to diet, etc., as circumstances would admit of, sufficed in most cases to remove the affection and restore the patient's strength.

As another of the sequelæ of fever, must be considered dropsical effusion into the cellular tissue which occurred most frequently after typhus and often to a very great extent.

It usually appeared the first week after convalescence had been established, in the feet and legs, gradually extending to the thighs, scrotum, cellular tissue of abdomen or even to the face; the skin became of a dusky brown hue, with livid patches interspersed; the limbs became tense and stiff and motion difficult and painful. *Phosphorus, Bryonia, Rhus* and *China* were the medicines generally used, and with tolerable success, particularly *Bryonia* and *Phosphorus.*

The total number of cases of fever treated (during sixty-seven days) was 111; of these twenty-four were typhus and eighty-seven continued fever.

Cases cured	108
Dismissed	1
Died	2
	111

Showing a mortality of 1.8 per cent, in the abstract a very low rate, but which will appear most striking when compared with the results of Allopathic practice in the same place, even with the advantages of hospital accommodation, attendance, proper food and drink, etc.

During the months of May, June and July, the total number of cases of fever treated in the Bantry Union Hospital was 254, of these 35 died, showing a mortality of 13.8 per cent, which forms a striking contrast to that under Homœopathic treatment (1.8 per cent).

The returns of the Bantry Hospital could not be obtained for April, (the worst month of the four), owing to the confusion caused by the crowded state of the house and the illness of one of the medical attendants at that time.

DYSENTERY

The principal cause of this disease may be clearly traced to the abrupt change which took place in the dietary of the people, from potatoes and milk and occasionally fish and meat to the almost unvaried use of Indian Meal, owing to the extravagant prices of the other farinaceous articles of food (flour, oatmeal etc.), and to the scarcity of milk, from the fatality amongst cattle during the winter.

That Indian meal is a nutritious article of food, is undeniable (particularly well fitted for those at active labour) but it is equally undeniable that it was the cause of much suffering and disease, which may in a great measure be ascribed to its improper preparation, the grain being very coarsely ground, with the bran generally unseparated (which is far more irritating than the bran of wheaten flour), and the meal thus obtained used either boiled in water or made into hard flat cakes, in either mode alike indigestible.

The actual change of diet must also be considered as a powerful cause, for in previous years the supply of potatoes generally fell short, in most parts of Ireland during June and July when oatmeal became the ordinary article of diet amongst the poor, at which time every Dispensary physician in the country districts had an unusual amount of cases of gastric affections applying for treatment. These causes combined, *the change to a diet of indigestible, badly cooked food, insufficient in quantity, with a general state of mental and physical depression*, may be considered as the origin of Dysentery.

In order to study its nature and symptoms with more accuracy and satisfaction, three sub-divisions or groups may be distinguished and called 1st, the acute Dysentery; 2nd, the ordinary form as it attacked adults; and 3rd, as it appeared in children; this division being not merely artificial, but the natural arrangement which suggested itself to my mind at the time and which was constantly acted upon in practice.

1st The symptoms of the first group generally came on suddenly, with excruciating, griping, cutting or shooting pains all over the abdomen, most severe about the umbilical region, with soreness and pain upon pressure; and cutting, forcing and excruciating pain at rectum, with tenesmus and straining after the evacuations, which were most frequent, once or twice every hour, scanty, yellowish or brownish, mixed with blood in large proportion

93

(constipation sometimes preceded), expression of intense anguish and anxiety on the countenance, with rapid exhaustion; hiccough, thirst, vomiting, small, weak, rapid intermittent pulse; its progress was very rapid and frequently towards a fatal termination.

As instances of this division, I shall read the details of two cases transcribed from my note book.

CASE I

J.M., aged about forty years, of a thin, spare habit and dark complexion, visited April 27th, the seventh day of Dysentery. Complains of violent shooting pains about umbilicus and along the course of colon, with soreness to the touch, and forcing, cutting, kneady pain at anus after each evacuation, the number of these being about fifteen to twenty in the twenty-four hours, very scanty, mixed with much blood and mucus; tongue white and furred; skin hot, not dry; countenance expressive of intense anxiety and suffering, with constant moaning and crying.

Tinct. *Mercurius corrosivus* 5, gtt. iij., 1/15 omni hora.

May 1st – The soreness and shooting pain extremely severe, rather less pain at rectum.

Tinct. *Arsenicum album*, 3, gtt. iij. 1/12 2dis. horis.

3rd – No improvement.

Rept. *Arsenicum album,* at the same dose and interval.

6th – The pains have almost ceased, the motions much less frequent, slept well last night.

Rept. *Arsenicum album,* a dose every five hours.

9th – Continued improving till this day, when a slight return of the shooting pain occurred. He immediately took one of two doses of *Arsenicum album*, left with him against that occasion, and very quickly found relief.

10th – No pain today.

13th – No return of pain. Bowels quite regular.

(The effects of *Arsenicum album* were found very satisfactory in this case.)

CASE II
D.C., aged sixteen years, visited April 24th, seventh day of Dysentery. Complains of the most excruciating, cutting and burning pains at rectum, with straining and tenesmus after every evacuation, these evacuations consisting almost entirely of blood, scanty and fluid, very frequent, at least once every half-hour; pulse rapid and weak; skin moist; tongue covered with white fur; slight aching in the bones of the extremities; rapid failure of strength.
Tinct. *Mercurius corrosivus*, 5, gtt. iv. 1/12 omni hora.

26th – There is no improvement in any of the symptoms, the tenesmus and pain in the anus are rather more severe.
Tinct. *Mercurius corrosivus*, 5, gtt. iij.
Tinct. *Nux vomica,* 3, gtt. iij.
A dose of each (1/8) to be taken alternately every hour.

27th – Died this morning in great agony.

This was the most severe case of Dysentery met with in all my experience, and interested me very much during the three days it continued under treatment; the medicines seemed to have had no effect on the symptoms, which advanced with the utmost rapidity to a fatal termination.

2nd The ordinary form of Dysentery, as it attacked adults, generally commenced with loss of appetite, nausea and looseness of the bowels, which gradually increased, till in the course of four or five days all the urgent symptoms of Dysentery became developed.

The pain was generally very severe, most so before and after each evacuation, and described as 'cutting,' 'forcing,' 'smarting,' with tenesmus and straining, seldom with shooting pain across the umbilical region; evacuations from twelve to fifteen or twenty in the twenty-four hours, most frequent during the day; scanty, gelatinous, yellowish or brownish, streaked with blood, or consisting of two parts – a thin reddish serum with a tough, pale red, fibrinous-looking matter, in flakes or thread-like pieces, generally sinking to the bottom of the vessel; (where the evacuated matter was of the latter character the attendant pain was invariably extreme). For many minutes after each evacuation the patient suffered intense pain from tenesmus and straining, which in some cases produced *imperfect* prolapsus ani.

It was in this class of cases that the effects of *Mercurius corrosivus* and *Nux vomica* were best seen, given singly, in succession or alternately (according to each particular case), at intervals varying from two to six or eight hours. It was seldom found necessary to give *Aconite,* as the condition of the patient was rather the reverse of inflammatory, as indicated by slow and weak pulse, loss of strength etc. Where the pain was of a shooting character about the navel and the evacuations very little bloody, *Arsenicum album* or *Veratrum* were given, as also *Nux vomica* and with equally satisfactory results; occasionally *Rhus* or *China* were given towards the termination of the disease, when the symptoms were much changed.

Anasarca in the limbs or trunk occasionally accompanied and followed Dysentery in adults, and continued for some weeks after the healthy action in the intestines had been restored. The remedies used in it were almost the same as those previously described in the treatment of Dropsy following Fever.

CASE III
K. Mc C., aged forty-two years, visited April 28th, had been three weeks confined to bed with dysentery. Complains of acute shooting pain across umbilical region, with much flatulence, also of cutting pain at rectum, motions frequent (from ten to fifteen in twenty-four hours), scanty, thin, brownish, yellow, slightly streaked with blood, followed by painful tenesmus; extensive anasarca of the limbs and trunk, the former feel stiff and dead, almost incapable of motion.
Tinct. *Nux vomica,* 3 gtt. iij. 1/12 4tis horis.

May 1st – Motions less frequent, the pain unchanged.
Tinct. *Mercurius corrosivus* 5, gtt. iij. 1/8 5tis horis.

3rd – Much improved, but three or four evacuations in the twenty-four hours

with very little pain. No change in anasarca.
Tinct. *Bryonia,* 3, gtt. iij. 1/12 6tis horis.

7th – Bowels regular, no pain. The Dropsy has left the limbs and now appears in the face.
Rept. *Bryonia*

10th – She is up and able to walk.
To continue taking the *Bryonia* at intervals of twelve hours.

15th – The Dropsy has disappeared, the bowels continue regular.

CASE IV

J.N., aged twenty-two years, visited April 19th, seventh day of Dysentery. Complains of severe cutting and burning pain in rectum with straining and forcing before and during each motion, and tenesmus for several minutes after; evacuations from twenty to thirty in the twenty-four hours, most frequent during the day, scanty, consisting of a bloody mucous mixed with red fibrinous-like flakes; tongue covered with white fur; no appetite; pulse natural; skin cool. She is thirsty.
Tinct. *Mercurius corrosivus*, 5, gtt. iij. 1/15 2dis horis.

21st – Improving.– Rept. *Mercurius corrosivus*, a dose every four hours

24th – Motions about eight or ten in twenty-four hours,
brownish yellow, mixed with a little bloody mucous, followed by tenesmus and straining.
Tinct. *Mercurius corrosivus*, 5, gtt. iij. 1/10 4tis horis.

26th – Tenesmus much relieved. Complains of shooting pain across umbilical region.
Tinct. *Nux vomica,* 3 gtt. ij. 1/8 6tis horis

28th – Bowels almost regular.

30th – Up and out, feels quite well.

Dysentery, as it appeared in children from the ages of one year to twelve or fourteen, differed in many respects from the same disease in adults, being more difficult of cure and the symptoms more severe. The principal points of difference were in the *character of pain, and of evacuations, in the more frequent (almost universal) occurrence of prolapsus ani, in the enormous increase in development of the abdomen, the voracious appetite, the extreme degree of emaciation which ensued in most cases, the rare occurrence of anasarca, the higher ratio of mortality, and the predominance of symptoms at night.*

In children the disease generally commenced (after the long continued use of Indian meal) with looseness of the bowels, rather sudden in its access, attended with acute pain shooting across the umbilical region; or most usually, continual, dull gnawing, aching pain, referred to the region between the epigastrium and the umbilicus, with tenesmus and straining before and after each motion, which were in general not scanty, but thin, semi-fluid, greenish, yellowish or yellowish-brown, mixed with blood in various proportions and sometimes with slimy sanguinolent mucous. As the disease advanced, the pain below epigastrium became more severe, and the motions more frequent, prolapsus ani almost invariably followed. But the sense of tenesmus and the pain in rectum became less severe or disappeared, (from the sensibility of the mucous membrane becoming obtunded by the frequent exposure of the intestines?) the appetite became most voracious, which could not be satisfied but with improper food, and therefore aggravated the disease; the abdomen gradually became enlarged to a most surprising extent, which enlargement could not be owing either to flatulence or to effusion, as the surface was tense, slightly irregular and unyielding, emitting a dull sound on percussion, nor could the most careful examination detect fluctuation. The profuse evacuations would also prove that it could not be owing to accumulation of fæces in the intestines.

From physiological and pathological reasoning, it appeared to me to have arisen from an increase in actual development of the intestines, to accommodate themselves to an altered and increased action upon their surface, the consequence of the change of diet and of the voracious appetite; thus we frequently observe the intestinal canal of carnivorous animals to become developed almost equally to that in herbivorous (as when dogs have been for a long time fed on vegetable diet), and even in disease, (as in hypertrophy of the heart from valvular disease), increase of work given to an organ, causes increase of development.

The abdomen at this time presented a most peculiar appearance, like a section of an enormous oval applied to the trunk, which latter, the limbs being extremely emaciated, rendered the contrast more striking; by degrees the features became haggard and thin and emaciation advanced to such a degree that the limbs appeared like bones covered with skin alone or like dirty parchment drawn tightly over a solid support. In many instances, actual deformity and distortion of the lower extremities ensued, from defective nutrition of the osseous tissue and loss of muscular support.

The medicines found most useful in this class of cases were *Arsenicum album, Veratrum, Nux vomica, Mercurius corrosivus, Rhus, Sulphur, China, Secale.* In the early stages of the disorder, where violent cutting or shooting pain across the umbilical and iliac regions existed, with frequent, fluid evacuations, yellowish or brownish, and tinged with blood, small doses of *Veratrum* or *Arsenicum album* (Tinct.3) were given at intervals varying from two to six or eight hours, till symptoms of amelioration appeared or the character of the pain and evacuations changed.

In the early stages also, where severe cutting pain and tenesmus, prolapsus ani, etc. existed in addition to the shooting pain, *Nux vomica* or *Mercurius corrosivus* were given either singly or in alternation, more usually the former, and these in most cases *during the early stage* were found sufficient to effect a cure, and with tolerable rapidity.

In the second or chronic stage, where frequent, abundant evacuations, semi-fluid, with little or no blood, prolapsus ani, *without tenesmus or pain in ano*, voracious appetite, with enlargement of abdomen and increasing emaciation, dull gnawing pain below epigastrium were found the leading symptoms, *Nux vomica* and *Sulphur* were found the most serviceable and in most cases removed the symptoms; unless where the voracious appetite and use of improper food kept up so continual a state of irritation in the mucous membrane that no medicine could cure, without the more or less perfect removal of the cause.

In this stage of the disease, much benefit was also derived from *Arsenicum album* and *Rhus,* and in a lesser degree from *China, Secale,* etc. according to their particular indications.

CASE V

T.D., aged six years, visited April 13th, the sixth week of Dysentery. Tongue dry and white; pulse small, rapid and weak; evacuations about eight or ten in the twenty-four hours, brownish yellow and mixed with a little blood, fluid and not scanty, attended with sharp, shooting or cutting pain at times, day and night, about the umbilical region; no appetite, with distaste for food; much emaciation; short, hollow cough at night without expectoration.
Tinct. *Arsenicum album*, 3, gtt. iij. 1/12 6tis horis.

17th – Very little better, the pain still very severe.
Tinct. *Veratrum,* 3, gtt. ij, 1/12 3tiis horis.

19th – He is better. The motions not bloody, less frequent and with less pain.
Rept. *Veratrum,* a dose every five hours.
22nd – Continues improving, only the motions this day, with sharp pain about umbilicus
Arsenicum album, 12, 2 gt, 1/6 6tis horis.

24th – Bowels not moved since yesterday; rests well at night.
To continue *Arsenicum album.*

28th – Continues without any symptoms.

CASE VI

M.M., aged four years, visited first April 17th, third week of Dysentery. Complains of severe cutting pain at rectum; evacuations very frequent (twenty to thirty in twenty-four hours), abundant, semi-fluid, greenish yellow, mixed with bloody mucus, very offensive; tenesmus and straining after each evacuation, with painful prolapsus ani; tongue loaded with white fur; pulse weak, rapid and thready. She is very much emaciated, with a greenish white colour of the skin, which is dry and stiff.
Tinct. *Mercurius corrosivus,* 5, gtt. ij, 1/12 4tis horis.

21st – Motions less frequent (about ten of fifteen in the twenty-four hours), with very little blood and less pain; the prolapsus ani as before.
Tinct. *Nucis vomica,* 3, gtt. ij, 1/10 6tis horis.

24th – Motions still less frequent, (eight to twelve in twenty-four hours)
Rept. *Nux vomica*

28th – Improving; still prolapsus ani after each motion.
Tinct. *Mercurius corrosivus,* 5, gtt. ij, 1/8 6tis horis.

30th – But two or three motions this day, without pain and very little prolapsus ani.
To continue the *Mercurius corrosivus.*

May 3rd – Bowels almost regular. – No medicine

5th – No symptoms.

CASE VII
T.H., aged six years. He has been three months ill with Dysentery. Visited April 13th. Abdomen enormously enlarged, slightly irregular on the surface, hard and tense, without evidence of fluctuation. Constant dull, gnawing pain a little below the epigastrium with, at times, shooting pain along colon; evacuations about eight to ten in the twenty-four hours, thin, greenish and putrid, not bloody at present, (had been so before); tongue dry and white; skin dry and hard; pulse small and weak, rather slow; the body looks pale and emaciated, as if scarcely able to sustain the prominent abdomen. He has a constant craving for food.
Sulphur 12, gt. 3, 1/8 night and morning

17th – Very little change in the symptoms.
Nux vomica 12 gt. 3, 1/8 night and morning.

22nd – Motions becoming less frequent (two or three in the day), with less of the gnawing pain His appearance is also improving.
Rept. *Nux vomica*

25th – Bowels regular; no pain. The enlargement of abdomen remains the same.

The total number of cases of Dysentery treated, (including a few cases of Diarrhoea after Fever, that had not been under homœopathic treatment during the Fever) was 81; of these

34 were from the age of 1 to 16 years
27 were from the age of 16 to 30 years
11 were from the age of 50 to 70 years

Of the 34 young persons   6 died
Of the 27 adults   2 died
Of the 11 old people   3 died

which shows the mortality to have been highest in old people, next in the young, and far less in adults. The rate of mortality in the entire was 14 per cent, which when compared with the results of Allopathic treatment, appears equally satisfactory as those in Fever.

During May, June and July, 250 cases of Dysentery were treated in the Bantry Union Hospital, of these 90 died, or 35 per cent, thus showing a comparative mortality of 14 to 35 in favour of Homœopathic treatment, during a more unfavourable period. The return of the number of cases of fever and dysentery treated in the Bantry Union Hospital, and their results, were furnished me by one of the physicians of that institution, from the reports taken by the medical attendants at that time.

6 THE LAST ILLNESS OF LORD BEACONSFIELD
by Dr JOSEPH KIDD

When I commenced my attendance on Lord Beaconsfield in November 1878, he was in a sad condition of health, suffering from Bright's disease, bronchitis and asthma; at night his sleep much disturbed by cough, wheezing and breathlessness; suffering much all day from nausea – the result of *ipecacuanha* taken at night for the asthma – and from headache and gouty dyspepsia increased by the use of steel and port wine ordered for him because of his 'debility'. With a grim smile he often alluded to such a remedy for debility, and the pitiable results. The disturbed nights had also brought on depression of spirits, loss of appetite and unfitness for brain work. For the ipecacuanha and steel, *iodide of potassium* was substituted and subsequently a mild course of *arsenic* which cleared his bronchial tubes without any subsequent nausea. In place of the port wine the finest Chateau Lafite was given. Indigestion disappeared as a strict regimen was laid down and followed. The dinner became a light repast of one course, without pastry, pudding or fruit. He soon began to have a most hearty appetite for breakfast and lunch. He slept well at night without asthma, as he took less and less food at dinner.

The albuminuria (Bright's disease of the kidney) was wasting his strength and was much aggravated by the dry state of the skin. Regarding it as the most important indication for treatment, I advised the regular use of a lamp bath at bedtime for fifteen minutes, and to sleep in a nightdress and sheets of soft Saxony flannel. At first he rebelled at this. "You say you want me to perspire. I never did since I was born. I have had a dry skin all my life. It is useless for you to try." But he obeyed as I explained its importance for the relief of the kidneys and he allowed his faithful servant, Mr Baum, to administer the lamp bath regularly on alternate nights. I visited him three times a week, in the morning soon after nine for many months. As I felt his skin at each visit he would say quietly: "No use, give up the trial, you will never bring me to perspire." My answer was a quiet "Yes: by perseverance I will succeed, and to your great relief when I do." He was a very sharp observer of doctors, by many of whom he had been treated. To conquer in everything was his passion, yet he had no faith in any doctor who was easily moved from his own ground or could be driven to yield. About three months after this treatment was commenced at one of my morning visits, while I was feeling his skin carefully, he looked up with a most genial smile. 'You have conquered,' he said; "I perspired freely last night." Gradually his skin became soft like a child's and a gentle moisture all night added to the comfort of his life; the morning depression vanished and the albuminuria lessened, his old freshness and vigour returned. During the next few months the relief afforded was very helpful, the depression and weariness passed off, he was able to enjoy his work and take open air exercise. The improvement lasted all through 1879, with the exception of a feverish chill in November, which confined him to the house for a week.

He recovered well from this, seldom suffered from asthma, although obliged to keep very strictly to his diet regimen, as the least infraction gave him bad nights.

The greatest difficulty was to get the patient to take exercise. "My grand-father," he said to me, "lived to ninety years; he took much open air exercise. My father lived to eighty, yet he never took any." Lord Beaconsfield tried to steer a middle course, but the utmost he could be per-suaded to take was a short walk two or three times a week if Lord Rowton or some other pleasant friend called to accompany him, otherwise he easily found an excuse for not going out. His slow pace in walking prevented him from getting much benefit from it.[1] Riding he had given up, although in his

---

[1] At Constantinople in 1830 he was greatly gratified by a certain Mehemet Pasha telling him that he could not be an Englishman, but rather one of an Eastern race, because he walked so slowly. *Quarterly Review,* p23, January 1889

early days passionately devoted to it. For many years his life had been a sedentary one; presuming on his hardy constitution, and the fact of his father's great age without open air exercise, he considered it a matter optional in his case. He had the excuse of urgent occupation in his political and ordinary life to hinder it. yet Nature has a 'Nemesis' power of revenging herself on the man of sedentary life. In the end the liver suffers. In one of his letters to his sister he says: 'I have recovered from the horrors of a torpid liver which has overwhelmed me the last few days.'

The character of Lord Beaconsfield was most singular. To those without, his manner was that of reserve and coolness, with a proud expression of power and lofty aim. But to the charmed inner circle of his friends there was a bright genial glow of kindness shown which made all feel at ease. At first a manner apparently cold and distant, but directly you struck the chord of sympathy, most cordial and responsive.[2]

In the company of ladies his face became most animated. All the activity of his mind became freshened into new life and he spared neither time not trouble to interest them. An old lady, Mrs de Burgh, hearing of his asthma, sent him a pot of Stockholm tar, with a note advising him to expose it in his bedroom at might. It proved helpful. An ordinary Prime Minister in full work might have written an autographic note of thanks. Lord Beaconsfield found time to visit her in Eccleston Square to thank her for her kind present, much to her delight.

Through all the constant intercourse of nearly three years there was not a hitch or break in his Lordship's cordial manner to myself personally, except once. He was then suffering much from gout and irritability of liver. In striking contrast with his usual manner he was curt and sharp to me, but I knew it was only a symptom of his disease. *Yet the same evening* Mr Bernal Osborne sat next to Lord Beaconsfield at dinner, and the next day said to a friend of mine, 'During dinner Lord Beaconsfield spoke again and again to me of Dr Kidd and said, "I owe the health and comfort of my life and my fitness for work to his care." '

---

[2] In his latter years the expression of his eyes was marred by an unhealthy state of the mucous membrane of the eyelids which rather disfigured him.

After the London season his life at Hughenden was very quiet: a walk around the 'German Forest' – a lovely clump of young trees that Lord Lyndhurst named the 'German Forest' – and a look at the beautiful shrubs and trees on the Terrace, most of them with a history, one planted by this friend and one by that. he delighted to recall the memories of old friends from the trees planted by them. After his walk, to write or to read was his chief occupation. He was a great reader: of the many journals and reviews on his table, the *Revue Des Deux Mondes* was his favourite. Over it he spent much time.

At Hughenden he was the most genial of hosts. To interest me one evening there he took out a rare old copy of Virgil, and opened up its treasures till I began to share his enthusiasm. 'Dining here often alone,' he said to me, 'I have an understanding with my cook that there is to be ten minutes interval between one course and the next. That ten minutes I invariably devote to reading one of the great authors of antiquity, and I can say that for many years I have listened to many of the greatest wits and orators of the age, but I have derived more pleasure and enjoyment from Homer, Virgil and Horace than from all the living celebrities I have met in life.'

His general health gradually improved in 1879, with occasional interruptions. He kept steadily to the use of lamp baths, as he delighted in the relief through the skin. He had much more faith in wise general hygienic and dietetic treatment than in medicines.

As the time of the Berlin Conference drew near, Lord Rowton, his dearest and best friend, urged that I should accompany him to Berlin. Lord Beaconsfield was unwilling, satisfied with my promise to be in readiness to start at once for Berlin if telegraphed for. At Berlin his health was suddenly disturbed by a sever chill. An urgent telegram summoned me there. I found him suffering from a fresh attack of congestion of the kidneys and liver, but was enabled to afford prompt relief, and he recovered his usual vigour of mind and body, and got through the work of the Congress with ease. I remained with him till the Treaty of Berlin was completed, and returned with him as far as Calais. Three or four days before the Treaty was signed, I was sitting with him in his private room when Prince Bismarck was announced. He walked into the room giving his hat to the servant. After being introduced to the Prince, I retired and found the servant outside the door trying on Prince Bismarck's hat. 'Why,' said one of them, 'the hat is almost big enough to take our two heads into it.' The day after Lord Beaconsfield said to me 'I can tell you today the object of Bismarck's visit yesterday, as it is no longer a secret. The Congress was on the point of coming to an untimely end that morning, as I absolutely refused one of the Russian Plenipotentiary's conditions, and I left the Congress room saying I should have to return to London at once to concert other measures. Bismarck heard of this and rushed off to the Russian Ambassador, persuaded him to withdraw the point and then called to stop my return to London.'

At Berlin he was the favourite of the people, crowds waited outside his hotel to catch a glimpse of him, and as he walked out leaning on the arm of Lord Rowton, without police or soldiers, the crowds followed him with an expression of the deepest regard and interest. On his return from Berlin the King of the Belgians sent his own private saloon railway carriage to Berlin for Lord Beaconsfield's use and sent it on by special express from Brussels to Calais.

During the winter of 1880 his condition became more and more anxious, the frequent changes of temperature increasing the tendency to asthma which the Bright's disease intensified. The kidneys gradually became incompetent to remove waste products, leading to the accumulation within the body of substances (poisonous to the brain) that should have been eliminated by the kidneys. The bronchial cough became more and more troublesome and the expectoration difficult. The relief from the *iodide of potass* and the lamp bath became less, and a gradual deterioration of health supervened as the albumen increased, depression of spirits coming on with suppressed gout.

In the spring of 1881 he felt the cold most keenly, and seldom went out for a walk, his only exercise. Yet he could not deny himself the pleasure of going into society in the evening. He thought that with fur coats and shut carriage he might risk it. But on one of the worst nights in March he went out to dinner and returning home was caught for a minute by the deadly blast of the north-east wind laden with sleet. Bronchitis developed the next morning with distressing asthma, loss of appetite, fever and congestion of the kidneys. Notwithstanding prompt treatment he began to lose ground. Sleepless nights and weary days gradually undermined his strength, the deadly uraemia crept on. I visited him three times a day, and for a week sat up with him all night. The paroxysms of asthma came on so suddenly and violently that quick relief was needed. His constitution did not respond to the remedies as before.

Asthma is the most peculiar disease. It comes on often in the most healthy places and vanishes in the crowded close streets of the town. In the low-lying Downing Street near the Thames he had much less asthma than in Curzon Street, where his bedroom was a small stuffy one with fluffy paper and old-fashioned curtains. From the first asthma followed him in Curzon Street. After a week in the close small bedroom, the bed was moved out into the airy drawing-room with great benefit. On the tenth day of the attack, when the dangerous nature of his illness had declared itself, Dr. Quain and Dr Mitchell Bruce became associated with me in the treatment. Dr Bruce and I divided the watching at night, he taking on half the night, and I the rest. Thus the great strain on my mind and body was relieved. This was most welcome to the patient, as he wished to spare me after having had seven nights' close watching. The visits of Dr Quain were very highly appreciated by Lord Beaconsfield, who was much helped by his great skill and cheerful manner. He was ready to meet every symptom and suffering with a fresh suggestion and cheering word. One day, with a smile, Lord Beaconsfield said to the doctor, 'You have given a good report, but your face looks anxious.' Dr Mitchell Bruce' watchful care and attention proved invaluable, and were always gratefully welcomed.

During his last illness there was no pain nor acute suffering, but at times much distress and endurance. To all those around him he showed the greatest kindness and consideration. He watched the daily reports of his case in the newspapers. Thus it became an anxious duty every night at eleven o'clock to write out the bulletin for the morning papers. It was very difficult steering to give a true idea of the gravity of his illness without causing anxiety to him on reading it. This caused many an anxious hour to the three doctors.

During one of our eleven o'clock settlings of the bulletin H.R.H. the

Prince of Wales and H.R.H. the Duke of Edinburgh, fresh home from the funeral of the murdered Czar, came in upon us, asking anxiously of the progress of our illustrious patient. Amongst the many distinguished callers Mr Gladstone walked in and inquired most feelingly after his old opponent. We, the doctors, had a hard time in reading the many hundreds of letters, telegrams and postcards with suggestions for infallible cure. One card to Lord Beaconsfield delighted him much; it was:

Don't die yet; we can't do without you. (Signed) A British Workman.

Lord Beaconsfield's love and regard for Earl Cairns were unbounded. One day during his illness Lord Beaconsfield said to me, 'I want especially to see Lord Cairns. He is admirable in council, I want to explain my views to him.' After spending upwards of an hour with Lord Beaconsfield, Lord Cairns came out and said to me 'With so near a prospect of death, can you not get Canon Fleming to visit him? He is specially the one Lord Beaconsfield would listen to on matters concerning the soul and eternity.' Obstacles were put in the way, and the opportunity was lost. To myself sitting by his bed at night he spoke twice on spiritual subjects, on a manner indicating his appreciation of the work of Christ and of the Redemption. At Hughendon he was a diligent attendant at the communion service, and when in London at Whitehall Chapel.

All through his illness, till within a few days of the end, the heart's action was steady and regular; a good vigorous pulse showed the hardy race from which he descended; but even with a vigorously acting heart the outlook for a man at seventy-six is bad when the kidneys fail to eliminate the gout poison. Chronic disease of the kidneys renders the patient much more susceptible to chills and sudden changes of climate. The greatest care in clothing may lessen the effect of such, but the deadly undermining action goes on by the insensible wasting of the nutritive parts of the blood (the albumen) and the defective elimination of the saline debris of the tissues.

About a fortnight before he died I found him greatly exhausted after the exertion of getting out of bed. I asked him to allow the nurses to manage for him. 'No' he said, with a fixed determination, 'I must get out of bed.' Quietly yielding, I sent at once for a fracture couch and had it placed alongside the bed he was lying upon. When next he got out of bed, I asked him to come to the fracture couch in place of his bed. His delight was extreme, the ease with which it was raised up or let down and its soft padding relieved his wary limbs. The mechanical contrivance rendered the getting out of bed unnecessary. 'Conquered' he said, with a genial smile and a cordial grasp of the hand.

Towards the close his nights became much disturbed by coughing. The more he used what he called 'the little demon' (a powder of *saltpetre* and *stramonium* to burn up and fill his chest with vapour) the worse its after effects, the shorter became the relief and the more frequent the need to have recourse to it, exhaustion following it. Spite of all our efforts the kidneys became more and more deeply obstructed, the amount of albumen increased; but worse than that the excretion of urea became less and less, so that blood-poisoning (uræmia) insensibly gained ground, and the nervous system fed by poisoned blood became exhausted. The restlessness at night also became more distressing, and his strength gave way, thus the bronchial tubes became clogged with mucus which he was unable to expectorate. Although the utmost care was taken to keep the temperature of the rooms equable, towards the 18th of April a gradual change for the worse came on, increased restlessness, loss of strength, incoherence of speech, occasional delusion, restlessness alternating with the heavy sleep of coma, increased frequency of pulse and of respiration.

At midnight there was a visible change for the worse, and the heaviness gradually passed into the calm sleep of death. Lord Rowton remained up all night with Dr Mitchell Bruce and myself. At one o'clock we summoned Dr Quain, Lord Barrington and Sir Philip Rose to witness the end. Lord Barrington was the first to arrive, and at once joined Lord Rowton in a loving clasping of Lord Beaconsfield's right hand; his left hand was laid in mine. Soon afterwards Dr Quain arrived. It touched us all deeply to see the dying statesman rise up in the bed and lean forward in the way he used to when rising to reply in debate; his lips moved but no sound came. he fell back on the pillows, and in about ten minutes, without suffering or distress, his spirit passed away.

7 DISEASED POTATO
Solanum tuberosum aegrotans

MATERIA MEDICA AND REPERTORY EXTRACTIONS

CLARKE[1]

INTRO
Diseased potato.
Tincture of the affected tubers.

GENERALITIES
A peculiar and most offensive odor immediately perceived on
approaching the bed.
Cannot walk erect.
General and partial debility.
Debility, she is about to faint.
Weariness in all the limbs, on waking.
Pain as if bruised, in bed, preventing her from stirring.
Muscular pains excruciating.
Cold water (whether drinking it or washing with it) causes a sense of
oppression and shock.

CHARACTERISTICS
The 'Potato murrain' is characterized by 'the rapid putrescence of the
leaves and haulm, which is first indicated by the presence of a little

[1] John Henry Clarke, *Dictionary of homœopathic materia medica*, London,
Homœopathic Publishing Co, 3 volumes, 1900 & 1925

mould, Peronospora infestans, which preys upon the tissues, spreading rapidly in every direction.

The tubers also exhibit brown spots on their surface and within their tissues, and according to circumstances decay with greater or less rapidity' (Treas. of Bot.).

In 1846 the sudden inroad of this disease led to the fearful famine in Ireland, which resulted in the death of thousands.

Mure made the first proving of Sol-t-ae., using a potato 'in an entire state of decomposition, without, however, being completely rotten.' Effects of eating diseased potatoes, some of them fatal, have been observed, and these have been added to Mure's. The symptoms of the proving were pretty severe, and one of the most important — prolapse of the rectum — has been confirmed by the poisoning cases.

A man and three children ate boiled diseased potatoes, and among their symptoms were these: 'Pain of an acute character was referred to the region of the anus, which on examination was found perfectly patulous and exquisitely tender to the touch.

Two of the four patients had prolapsus ani, which was probably caused by the violent and ineffectual efforts to discharge the contents of the rectum. There had not been an evacuation of the bowels, nor had they passed water, except in drops and with extreme suffering, for six days.

On introducing the finger into the rectum, which caused acute pain, it was found that the intestine was completely filled, to within an inch of the orifice, with a solid substance.' The foul odor of the diseased potato is reproduced in the breath and body odor of the patients.

Lips cracked and raw, gums bleeding, tongue coated, thick, cracked, throat inflamed and ulcerated with sensation of something sticking in it or a fleshy growth.

In one poisoning case a condition of noma of left cheek was induced.

Peculiar Sensations are: Of water splashing on head, as if brain were leaping in skull (on stooping).

As of something sticking in throat.

As if there were a fleshy growth in throat.

As if a spring unrolled in left hypochondrium.

As if a hollow body were turning rapidly in chest.

Of stoppage in trachea.

Of something becoming detached from sacrum.

The urine has an oily pellicle.
Excruciating muscular pains.
The symptoms are worse by touch and pressure.
Headache is worse on waking, by smell of alcohol, walking at 5 p.m., sleeping, working (headache).
Cold water causes shock.

CLINICAL
Anus, prolapse of, patulous.
Breasts, painful.
Breath, offensive, Constipation. Epistaxis. Headache.
Ileus.
Irritability.
Menses, interrupted.
Noma.
Odor of body, offensive.
Pruritus vulva.
Rectum, prolapse of.
Scalp, painful.
Sciatica.
Scurvy.
Skin, darkness of.
Tenesmus.
Tongue, cracked.
Vertebra, pain in, pulsation in.

MIND
Quarrelsome, irritable mood.
Bad temper.
 An unintelligible expression irritates her so that she would like to break everything and bite her hands.
Dread of work.
Hypochondriac mood.
She wants to enjoy a change of scenery, &c.
She fancies she is miserable, and dwells much on the future.
Rises in the night imagining that there are thieves behind the curtain, but dares not look, asks others to do it.

Crowd of ideas.
His attention is easily disturbed by other things.

HEAD
Confusion.
Heat in head, evening.
Heaviness of the head, in the vertex, on stooping and then raising head again.
Catarrhal dulness of head, especially forehead.
Sensation on stooping as if brain leaping in skull.
Lancinations as if brain would burst open.
Sensation of water splashing in head.
Headache at noon, worse by the smell of spirits.
Head feels too heavy, she has to make an effort to support it.
Pressure above eyes, on waking.
In the forehead: violent pain, all day, stitching pain, with dulness of head, and disposition to fall forwards.
Slight beating in temples.
Sensation as if the hair would be torn out on vertex.
Painful sensitiveness of scalp and roots of hair, cannot bear combing, better after stirring about and talking.

EYES
Prickling about the lids, the surface of which is red.
Spasmodic contraction and twitching of left upper lid.
Burning in lids.
Prickling and burning in eyes.
Congestion of the conjunctiva.
Profuse lachrymation, on waking.
EARS
Ringing in the left ear.

NOSE
Repeated sneezing, followed by feeble cough.
Nose-bleed.
Pressure at root of nose.
Smell of blood.

FACE

Face hot and red.

Mounting of heat to face, now and then.

Red pimples on cheeks.

Desquamation of face.

Face pale, bloodless, much swollen, especially about eyelids, nearly closing them.

Bluish-black, fetid ulcer of left cheek.

Upper lip bleeding, cracked.

MOUTH

Dry mouth.

The mucous membrane of the velum palati seems to become detached here and there.

Tongue pale.

Thick tongue, 2 A.M.

Tongue swollen, cracked, early in the morning, coated white or yellowish white, or coated white, with red tip, or yellowish along the median line.

Breath horribly fetid.

TEETH

Swelling of mucous membrane of the inner margin of the two incisors.

Teeth loose and very painful.

Gums, especially lower, spongy, oozing blood.

Teeth covered with white mucus.

THROAT

Mucus accumulates in throat and seems to cover whole anterior part.

Feeling as of a fleshy growth in throat.

Feeling as if something sticking in throat which she cannot bring up, followed by expectoration of a small, hard, yellowish-grey lump.

Fauces and mouth inflamed, ulcerated in patches.

Inflamed fauces, unable to swallow saliva.

STOMACH

Eructations followed by rumbling in stomach.

Sour eructations causing a cough.
Acidity, bitterness, and gulping-up, after eating.
Cardialgia after breakfast, dinner and supper.
Pain in stomach, with red face, after breakfast.
Spasmodic pains, griping-tearing at night.

APPETITE
Canine hunger.
Salt taste.
Taste of raw potatoes.
Food tastes as bitter as gall.
Great desire for spirits and oranges.
Burning thirst.

ABDOMEN
Sensation as if a spring were unrolled in left hypochondrium.
Pains and working in the bowels, early in the morning.
Painfulness of abdomen to contact along the median line.
Belly hard, swollen, dropsical.
In abdomen: pain after eating, spasmodic pains, as though the bowels became twisted together, dull pains in the hypogastric region, at night, pain with chilliness, rumbling, the clothes cause a feeling of tightness.
Emission of flatulence, also with colic.
Pain, as if sprained, in right groin.
Stitch in right groin near inguinal ring.

STOOL
Frequent urging to stool.
Stool scanty, with straining, passing off in small, black lumps (balls).
Has to strain until tears come.
Hard, large, lumpy stool, with violent burning in anus and rectum.
Stool hard and large, followed by two liquid stools.
Copious greenish-yellow diarrhoeic stool.
Constipation for five days.
Violent colic previous to stool.
Alternate protrusion and retraction of rectum during stool, with feeling of chilliness of body.

Prolapsus recti.

After stool rectum alternately falls and returns again.

Contraction of sphincter ani.

Strong pulsations in perineum and right ring finger.

Acute pain in anus, which was found perfectly patulous and exquisitely tender.

Great heat in anus.

URINARY

Region of bladder distended.

Difficult micturition.

Heat (and pain) in urethra after urinating.

Constant micturition while at stool.

Urine reddish, mingled with mucus.

Urine: very thick, becoming covered with white mucus after standing, soapy, turbid, of a dingy yellow, with copious white sediment, turbid, dingy yellow, covered with an oily pellicle.

Pain in urethra, after urinating.

MALE

Weight in right testicle all day.

FEMALE

Twisting pains through uterus.

Feeling of dislocation in hip-joint with pain in womb after a slight exertion.

Flatulence presses on uterus.

Menstrual blood rose-colored.

Suppression of the menses.

Menses smelling of foul fish, mixed with black coagula.

Small pimples and intolerable itching of labia.

Spasmodic pains striking through uterus.

Burning and itching in vagina.

RESPIRATORY

Constriction and difficulty of breathing, caused by dryness of mouth.

Hoarseness on walking.

In trachea: tearing, prickling, with cough, tearing, with phlegm, sensation as of an obstacle, followed by cough and expectoration of a lump of hard, yellowish-grey mucus.

Cough with expectoration of yellow mucus, at night.

Dry cough, day and night.

Cough as from stoppage in pharynx.

Expectoration of lumps of black blood, early in the morning.

Constant involuntary sighing.

After eating choking and difficult breathing caused by dryness of mouth.

Suffocation owing to previous day's dinner not digesting well, has to rise 3 A.M.

CHEST

Oppression in chest after supper.

Tearing in chest, also with dryness of mouth.

Sensation on making the least motion, as though a hollow body were turning rapidly round in chest quickly and with a noise, after which she fancies she will faint, early in morning.

Prickling as from a thousand pins on the inner surface of sternum.

Violent stitching pain above right breast.

Congestions to chest.

Acute pain in left side, like a stitch.

Painful stitches in right side.

Mammae painful, especially when raising arm.

HEART

Weight and pain in heart region.

Lancinations in heart.

Palpitation of heart: for moments, at night, when lying, when raising oneself, as though the heart would turn, with fainting feeling, with oppression of chest (less when lying), irregular (after eating).

Pulse: irregular, sometimes weak, hard and tense.

BACK & NECK

Swelling of muscles of neck, shoulders, and arms with pain so acute he winces on slightest pressure.

Sense of weight in the back part of the neck.

Violent beating in spine, early, when lying.

Prickling sensation in spine, during sleep, waking her.

Stinging pain in the large dorsal muscle, right side, when drawing breath.

Burning and painful sensation on the fifth dorsal vertebra, caused by friction of the clothes.

Sensation of weariness in whole back.

Stiffness in muscles of back.

Sensation as if something on the os-sacrum became detached.

Pain in sacrum, when walking or touching the part.

Tingling in sacrum.

Beating in right shoulder.

Prickling in psoas muscles.

Violent beating in loins.

Pain in lumbar vertebra, impeding walking.

Intolerable pain in lumbar region, obliging her to walk beat.

EXTREMITIES

Joints swollen and very painful.

Sense of weariness in all the limbs on waking.

Inclination to stretch the limbs.

UPPER LIMBS

Feeling of weariness in muscles posteriorly.

Pain as if sprained in right upper arm, after leaning on elbow.

Beating in middle portion of triceps brachealis.

(Cannot clench hands.)

Heat in hands.

Stinging in left little finger.

Beating in right ring finger.

LOWER LIMBS

Acute pains in hip-joint caused by least motion.

Painful pressure on hip-joint, as with an iron bar, compelling her to lie down.

In left gluteus muscle: beating, pain, accompanied by loathing.

Lancinations in posterior part of right thigh.

Weary feeling in muscles of right side, after walking.

Feeling of dislocation in hip-joint, with pain in womb, after a slight exertion.

Shooting pain in posterior and inferior femoral muscles, when bending knee.

Beating in internal femoral muscles.

Alternate beating and throbbing above patella in both limbs.

Pain as if sprained in whole vertebral column, striking through posterior parts of thigh, and extending down to heels.

Drawing pain in posterior part of right lower limb, from gluteus muscle down to heel.

Legs edematous.

Shuddering of right leg.

SLEEP

Irresistible drowsiness.

Very sleepy in evening.

Restless sleep.

Starting from sleep, as in a fright.

Sleepless.

Confused dreams, about fires, revolution, corpses, thieves, &c.

Amorous dream.

He dreams that he is to dress or draw the body of a drowned person, but is prevented in consequence of the body falling all the time on the clothes or paper.

Dreams about men who become transformed to talking animals, that his hands are cut to pieces, that he is falling from a steeple.

She dreams that she is eating human flesh, that she is swimming in a river, and cannot get out of it.

FEVER

Pulse irritated, irregular, hard and tense.

Chilliness and sensation of internal coldness.

Repeated chilly creepings through whole body, in evening.

Feeling of coldness all over, unable to get warm, her cheeks being very red, in afternoon.

Heat all over, with sweat.

Pyrexia, and afterwards dropsical appearance.

Violent paroxysms of heat, suddenly passing through the whole body, and proceeding from the vertex.

Alternate burning heat and chilliness, at night, in bed.

Exhalations from the skin, when performing the least work.

Sweat all over, early is morning, in bed, cold night-sweat.

The sweat smells of potatoes, in bed.

SKIN

Skin over whole body tender, tumefied, and preternaturally dark.

Rose-colored patches appear and as suddenly vanish.

Small pimples on the back, causing a violent itching.

Small red pimples on cheeks.

The skin in the face peels off a little.

Small pimples on back causes violent itching.

RELATIONSHIPS

Mure gives the following as the closest analogues of Sol-t-ae. the order indicates their relative importance: Bry., Ars., Plb., Nux-v., Sep., Stront., Viol-t., Squill., Puls., Graph., Alum., Merc., Nat-m., Ign., Calc.

Compare: Sensation of machinery inside, Nit-ac. Constipation, black balls, Op. Prolapsus ani, Podo., Ruta. Patulous anus, Apis., Phos.

ROBERTS Sensations as if [2]

BRUISED: IN BED, WHOLE BODY WERE.

Burst: head would.

Burst: brain would.

LEAPING IN SKULL ON MOTION, BRAIN WERE.

Torn: out on vertex, hair would be.

WATER: SPLASHING IN HEAD, WATER WERE.

Loose: teeth were.

POTATOES, TASTE OF RAW.

---

[2] Herbert A Roberts *Sensations as if: a repertory of subjective symptoms,* Philadelphia, Boericke & Tafel, 1937

TASTE: POTATOES, RAW.
Body: foreign, in throat.
GROWTH: IN THROAT, THERE WERE A FLESHLY.
Sticking: in throat, something were.
Stitches: in throat causing cough.
STOPPAGE IN PHARYNX.
Sprained: in right groin.
TWISTED: TOGETHER, BOWELS BECOME.
SPRING WERE UNROLLED IN LEFT HYPOCHONDRIUM.
Contracted: in anus.
DISLOCATION OF HIP JOINT WITH PAIN IN UTERUS.
MILK: WOULD RUSH IN AS WHEN CHILD NURSES.
STOPPAGE IN TRACHEA.
BODY: A HOLLOW, WERE TURNING RAPIDLY IN.
PINS: THOUSAND, PRICKING ON INNER SURFACE OF STERNUM.
Turn over, heart would.
TURNING: AROUND RAPIDLY, HEART WERE.
DETACHED FROM SACRUM, SOMETHING BECAME.
SPRAINED: IN WHOLE VERTEBRAL COLUMN.
SPRAINED: IN UPPER ARM.
BAR: OF IRON PRESSING ON HIP JOINT.
IRON: BAR WERE PRESSING ON HIP JOINT.
PRESSING: ON HIP JOINT, AN IRON BAR WERE.

WARD Sensations as if [3]

Acute pain as if the sacrum was out of place.
At the least movement she feels as if something hollow were turning rapidly round in the chest, with a rattling noise.
Burning thirst, as though her mouth were salt.
Cough, as if from obstruction of the pharynx.

---

[3] James Ward, *Unabridged dictionary of the sensations as if*, San Francisco, Wobbers Inc., 1939

Fearful colic as if the bowels were violently twisted, followed by a hard, copious stool.

Feeling as if sprained in the hip joint causing a pain in the uterus.

Feeling as of something sticking in the throat that she cannot bring up, followed by the expectoration of a small yellowish-gray lump.

Feels as if there was a fleshy growth in the throat.

Lancinations as if the brain would burst open, when going upstairs.

Pain as if from penknife stabs in the posterior portion of the right leg.

Pain as if from weariness, in the whole back and the posterior muscles of the thigh and arms.

Pain as if from weariness, in the whole back and the posterior muscles of the thighs and arms.

Pain as if sprained all along the spine, and running down the posterior muscles of the lower limbs, as far as the toes.

Pain as if sprained in the back part of the right hip-joint.

Pain as if sprained, in the right shoulder-joint after resting on the elbow in the evening in bed.

Pressure as if from an iron bar, upon the sacro-lumbar articulation.

Pricking as if with thousands of pins, on the right side of the internal surface of the sternum.

Pricking when asleep, as if pins were thrust into the spinal marrow which awakens her.

Ringing in the ears, as if she were going to faint.

Sensation as if a spring were enrolled in the left hypochondrium.

Sensation as of water splashing in the head.

Sensation as though something would become detached from the sacrum.

Sensation when stooping, as if the brain were leaping in the skull.

Strong palpitations of the heart, it was irregular, stopping for a moment and then returning with increased vigor, like a vessel suddenly uncorked.

The head and especially the forehead, are confused as if during a coryza.

The mucous membrane of the palate feels as if coming off in different places.

COMPLETE REPERTORY[4]
UNIQUE RUBRRICS

MIND; DREAMS; actors, turning black, green and yellow
MIND; DREAMS; body, body parts; hands; cut to pieces, being
MIND; DREAMS; cities; destroyed by fire
MIND; DREAMS; eating; human flesh
MIND; DREAMS; fire; destroying a city
MIND; DREAMS; magic
MIND; DREAMS; men; green and covered with moss, living in water, changing into dogs
MIND; DREAMS; men; transforming into talking animals
MIND; DREAMS; water; swimming in; get out, and cannot
MIND; DREAMS; witches
MIND; DREAMS; women; changed into animals
MIND; INDOLENCE, aversion to work; evening; ten pm.
MIND; IRRITABILITY; expression, from unintelligible
MIND; THOUGHTS; past, of the; journeys
MIND; THOUGHTS; rush, flow of; afternoon; five pm.
MIND; THOUGHTS; wandering; listening, while
MIND; THOUGHTS; wandering; work, at
MIND; WORK; aversion to mental; evening; eight pm.
HEAD; HEAT; Vertex; extending downwards
HEAD PAIN; GENERAL; odors; alcohol, of
HEAD PAIN; LANCINATING; Forehead; afternoon
EAR; NOISES in; ringing; faint, as if she was going to
NOSE; SNEEZING; ascending stairs agg.
ABDOMEN; PAIN; twisting; evening; ten thirty pm.
ABDOMEN; SPRING were unrolled in left hypochondrium, as if
RECTUM; TUMORS; decayed potato, like
FEMALE; ITCHING; afternoon
FEMALE; MENSES; bright red; nine am.

---

[4] David Kent Warkentin, *MacRepertory™and ReferenceWorks™*, Kent Homeopathic Associates, San Rafael, 1995
Roger van Zandvoort, *Complete Repertory,* IRHIS, Leidschendam, 1995

COUGH; DRY; midnight; before; ten thirty pm.
COUGH; SHRILL; waking, on
CHEST; PALPITATION heart; morning; seven am.
CHEST; PALPITATION heart; swallowing
BACK; PRICKLING; sleep, during
EXTREMITIES; PULSATION; Buttocks, nates; four pm.
SLEEP; SLEEPINESS; evening; seven thirty pm.
SLEEP; SLEEPLESSNESS; pains, from; joints, in
GENERALITIES; PAIN; sore, bruised; motion, on; bed, in

COMPLETE REPERTORY
ALL RUBRICS

MIND; ANXIETY; future, about
MIND; ANXIETY; waking, on
MIND; BREAK things, desire to
MIND; CENSORIOUS, critical
MIND; DELUSIONS, imaginations; thieves, robbers, sees
MIND; DELUSIONS, imaginations; thieves, robbers, sees; house, in
MIND; DESTRUCTIVENESS
MIND; DREAMS; actors, turning black, green and yellow
MIND; DREAMS; amorous
MIND; DREAMS; blood
MIND; DREAMS; blood; pools of
MIND; DREAMS; body, body parts; hands; cut to pieces, being
MIND; DREAMS; cities; destroyed by fire
MIND; DREAMS; confused
MIND; DREAMS; dead; bodies
MIND; DREAMS; disconnected
MIND; DREAMS; drowning; drowning man, of a
MIND; DREAMS; eating; human flesh
MIND; DREAMS; events; previous
MIND; DREAMS; events; previous; day, of
MIND; DREAMS; falling
MIND; DREAMS; falling; high places, from
MIND; DREAMS; fights

MIND; DREAMS; fire
MIND; DREAMS; fire; destroying a city
MIND; DREAMS; hemoptysis, spitting blood
MIND; DREAMS; hemorrhage
MIND; DREAMS; lewd, lascivious, voluptuous
MIND; DREAMS; ludicrous
MIND; DREAMS; magic
MIND; DREAMS; men; green and covered with moss, living in water, changing into dogs
MIND; DREAMS; men; transforming into talking animals
MIND; DREAMS; religious
MIND; DREAMS; vexatious
MIND; DREAMS; water
MIND; DREAMS; water; swimming in
MIND; DREAMS; water; swimming in; get out, and cannot
MIND; DREAMS; witches
MIND; DREAMS; women; changed into animals
MIND; FEAR; robbers, of
MIND; INDOLENCE, aversion to work; evening; ten pm.
MIND; IRRITABILITY
MIND; IRRITABILITY; expression, from unintelligible
MIND; LOQUACITY; evening
MIND; MEMORY; active; things done, read or seen, for
MIND; MOROSE, cross, fretful, ill-humor, peevish
MIND; RESTLESSNESS, nervousness; night
MIND; SADNESS, despondency, depression, melancholy
MIND; STARTING, startled; sleep; during
MIND; THOUGHTS; past, of the; journeys
MIND; THOUGHTS; rush, flow of; afternoon; five pm.
MIND; THOUGHTS; wandering; listening, while
MIND; THOUGHTS; wandering; work, at
MIND; WORK; aversion to mental; evening; eight pm.
HEAD; HEAT; Vertex; extending downwards
HEAD; SENSITIVENESS of Scalp or Brain; brushing hair, from
HEAD PAIN; GENERAL; night; amel.
HEAD PAIN; GENERAL; odors; alcohol, of
HEAD PAIN; LOCALIZATION; Forehead; daytime

HEAD PAIN; LOCALIZATION; Forehead; afternoon
HEAD PAIN; LANCINATING; Forehead; afternoon
HEAD PAIN; PRESSING; Forehead; eyes; over
HEAD PAIN; SORE, bruised, sensitive to pressure
EYE; LACHRYMATION; stool, during
EAR; NOISES in; ringing
EAR; NOISES in; ringing; faint, as if she was going to
NOSE; SNEEZING; ascending stairs agg.
FACE; DISCOLORATION; red
FACE; ERUPTIONS; pimples
FACE; ERYSIPELAS
FACE; HEAT; afternoon; four pm.
FACE; PAIN; General, aching, prosopalgia
MOUTH; ODOR, breath; putrid
THROAT; FOREIGN body, sensation of
THROAT; INFLAMMATION
THROAT; LUMP, plug, sensation of
THROAT; MUCUS
THROAT; PAIN; tearing
THROAT; ULCERS
STOMACH; APPETITE; wanting
STOMACH; ERUCTATIONS; General
STOMACH; ERUCTATIONS; General; evening
STOMACH; ERUCTATIONS; sour
STOMACH; HEAVINESS
STOMACH; PAIN; General
STOMACH; THIRST
STOMACH; TWISTING; breakfast, after
STOMACH; TWISTING; dinner, after
STOMACH; UNEASINESS
ABDOMEN; DISTENSION
ABDOMEN; DROPSY, ascites
ABDOMEN; FLATULENCE; evening
ABDOMEN; HARDNESS
ABDOMEN; ILEUS, paralysis of intestines
ABDOMEN; NOISES; rumbling
ABDOMEN; PAIN; general

ABDOMEN; PAIN; general; night
ABDOMEN; PAIN; general; diarrhea; before
ABDOMEN; PAIN; general; eating; after
ABDOMEN; PAIN; general; waking, on
ABDOMEN; PAIN; general; Hypogastrium
ABDOMEN; PAIN; general; Hypogastrium; morning
ABDOMEN; PAIN; lancinating; Iliac region
ABDOMEN; PAIN; sore, bruised, tenderness
ABDOMEN; PAIN; sore, bruised, tenderness; pressure, on; agg.
ABDOMEN; PAIN; twisting
ABDOMEN; PAIN; twisting; evening; ten thirty pm.
ABDOMEN; SPRING were unrolled in left hypochondrium, as if
RECTUM; CONSTIPATION
RECTUM; CONSTRICTION, closure, contraction
RECTUM; FLATUS; evening
RECTUM; FLATUS; night
RECTUM; HEAT; stool; after
RECTUM; OPEN anus
RECTUM; PAIN; burning; stool; after
RECTUM; PAIN; soreness
RECTUM; PAIN; tenesmus
RECTUM; PROLAPSE
RECTUM; PROLAPSE; stool; after
RECTUM; TUMORS; decayed potato, like
RECTUM; URGING, desire
RECTUM; URGING, desire; stool; after
STOOL; ODOR; offensive
FEMALE; ITCHING
FEMALE; ITCHING; afternoon
FEMALE; ITCHING; intolerable
FEMALE; MENSES; black
FEMALE; MENSES; bright red; nine am.
FEMALE; MENSES; clotted, coagulated
FEMALE; MENSES; frequent, too early, too soon
FEMALE; MENSES; intermittent
FEMALE; MENSES; offensive
FEMALE; MENSES; offensive; fish, like spoiled

LARYNX & TRACHEA; TICKLING in the air passages; Larynx, in
SPEECH & VOICE; VOICE; hoarseness; rising; after
SPEECH & VOICE; VOICE; hoarseness; waking, on
RESPIRATION; IRREGULAR
COUGH; DAYTIME
COUGH; AFTERNOON; five pm.
COUGH; EVENING
COUGH; NIGHT
COUGH; MIDNIGHT; before; ten thirty pm.
COUGH; DRY
COUGH; DRY; daytime
COUGH; DRY; evening
COUGH; DRY; night
COUGH; DRY; midnight; before; ten thirty pm.
COUGH; DRY; waking, on
COUGH; ERUCTATIONS; excite
COUGH; SHRILL
COUGH; SHRILL; waking, on
COUGH; SLEEP; wakens from
COUGH; STITCHING, from; larynx, in, from
COUGH; WAKING, on
EXPECTORATION; MORNING
EXPECTORATION; BLOODY, spitting of blood; morning
EXPECTORATION; GRAYISH
EXPECTORATION; LUMPY
CHEST; PAIN; General; Mammae
CHEST; PAIN; General; Heart; region of
CHEST; PALPITATION heart; morning; seven am.
CHEST; PALPITATION heart; noon
CHEST; PALPITATION heart; night
CHEST; PALPITATION heart; bed, on going to
CHEST; PALPITATION heart; motion
CHEST; PALPITATION heart; swallowing
BACK; PRICKLING
BACK; PRICKLING; sleep, during
EXTREMITIES; CLENCHING; Fingers
EXTREMITIES; CRAMPS; Thigh

EXTREMITIES; HEAT; Hand
EXTREMITIES; HEAT; Lower Limbs
EXTREMITIES; PULSATION; Shoulder
EXTREMITIES; PULSATION; Fingers; third
EXTREMITIES; PULSATION; Buttocks, nates
EXTREMITIES; PULSATION; Buttocks, nates; four pm.
EXTREMITIES; RAISED; Upper limbs; impossible to raise
EXTREMITIES; SWELLING; Joints
EXTREMITIES; SWELLING; Lower Limbs
EXTREMITIES; TENSION; Leg; calf
EXTREMITIES; WEAKNESS; General; waking, on
EXTREMITIES; WEAKNESS; Thigh; walking; after
EXTREMITY PAIN; JOINTS
EXTREMITY PAIN; JOINTS; walking; after
EXTREMITY PAIN; LOWER LIMBS; Buttocks, nates
EXTREMITY PAIN; BURNING; Hand
EXTREMITY PAIN; DRAWING; Leg
EXTREMITY PAIN; SPRAINED, as if; Hip
SLEEP; DISTURBED
SLEEP; DISTURBED; heat, by
SLEEP; LIGHT
SLEEP; RESTLESS
SLEEP; SLEEPINESS; evening; seven thirty pm.
SLEEP; SLEEPINESS; evening; eight pm.
SLEEP; SLEEPINESS; overpowering
SLEEP; SLEEPLESSNESS
SLEEP; SLEEPLESSNESS; morning
SLEEP; SLEEPLESSNESS; pains, from; joints, in
PERSPIRATION; HEAT; during
PERSPIRATION; ODOR; offensive
GENERALITIES; COLD; agg.
GENERALITIES; FAINTNESS, fainting
GENERALITIES; FAINTNESS, fainting; tendency to
GENERALITIES; FOOD and drinks; alcohol; desires
GENERALITIES; FOOD and drinks; coffee; desires
GENERALITIES; FOOD and drinks; oranges; desires
GENERALITIES; FOOD and drinks; stimulants; desires

GENERALITIES; MOON; agg.; full
GENERALITIES; PAIN; Bones
GENERALITIES; PAIN; Joints, of
GENERALITIES; PAIN; sore, bruised
GENERALITIES; PAIN; sore, bruised; motion, on; bed, in
GENERALITIES; PAIN; stitching; right side
GENERALITIES; PULSE; excited
GENERALITIES; PULSE; frequent, accelerated, elevated, exalted, fast, innumerable, rapid
GENERALITIES; PULSE; frequent, accelerated, elevated, exalted, fast, innumerable, rapid; small, and
GENERALITIES; PULSE; hard
GENERALITIES; PULSE; irregular
GENERALITIES; PULSE; small
GENERALITIES; PULSE; strong
GENERALITIES; PULSE; tense
GENERALITIES; PULSE; thready
GENERALITIES; PULSE; weak
GENERALITIES; SCURVY, scorbutus

Destruction

1. MIND; BREAK things, desire to
2. MIND; DESTRUCTIVENESS
3. MIND; DREAMS; body, body parts; hands; cut to pieces, being
4. MIND; DREAMS; fire
5. MIND; DREAMS; fights
6. MIND; DREAMS; fire; destroying a city

Tables of rubrics from *The Complete Repertory* by Michael Thompson

Blood

1. MIND; DREAMS; blood ☐
2. MIND; DREAMS; blood; pools of ☐
3. MIND; DREAMS; hemoptysis, spitting blood ☐
4. MIND; DREAMS; hemorrhage ☐
5. EXPCTORATION; BLOODY, sspitting of blood; morning ☐

Transformation

1. MIND; DREAMS; actors, turning black, green and yellow ☐
2. MIND; DREAMS; magic ☐
3. MIND; DREAMS; men; green and covered with moss, living in water, changing into dogs ☐
4. MIND; DREAMS; men; transforming into talking animals ☐
5. MIND; DREAMS; women; changed into animals ☐
6. MIND; DREAMS; witches ☐
7. GENERALITIES; MOON; agg.; full ☐

Death

1. MIND; DREAMS; dead; bodies ■
2. MIND; DREAMS; drowning; drowning man, of a ■
3. MIND; DREAMS; eating; human flesh ■

Water

1. MIND; DREAMS; drowning; drowning man, of a ■
2. MIND; DREAMS; water ■
3. MIND; DREAMS; water; swimming in ■
4. MIND; DREAMS; water; swimming in; get out, and cannot ■

Robbers

1. MIND; DELUSIONS, imaginations; thieves, robbers, sees
2. MIND; DELUSIONS, imaginations; thieves, robbers, sees; house, in
3. MIND; FEAR; robbers, of

Decay

1. MOUTH; ODOR, breath; putrid
2. RECTUM; TUMORS; decayed potato, like
3. STOOL; ODOR; offensive
4. FEMALE; MENSES; offensive
5. FEMALE; MENSES; offensive; fish, like spoiled
6. PERSPIRATION; ODOR; offensive
7. GENERALITIES; SCURVY, scorbutus

Strange

1. MIND; DREAMS; confused ▨
2. MIND; DREAMS; disconnected ▨
3. MIND; DREAMS; ludicrous ▨

The Past

1. MIND; DREAMS; events; previous ▨
2. MIND; DREAMS; events; previous; day, of ▨
3. MIND; MEMORY; active; things done, read or seen, for ▨
4. MIND; THOUGHTS; past, of the; journeys ▨

8 SOURCES

T F Allen, *Encyclopaedia of pure materia medica*, Philadelphia, Boericke & Tafel 1879

William Boericke & Oscar Boericke, *Pocket manual of homœopathic materia medica*, Philadelphia, Boericke & Runyon 1927

Roseline Brillat, *Benoît Mure, missionaire de l'homéopathie, 1809-1858*, Lyon, Éditions Boiron, 1988

Jacques Baur, *Un livre sans frontières; histoire et métamorphose de l'Organon de Hahnemann*, Lyon, Éditions Boiron, 1991

Thomas Lindsley Bradford, *Pioneers of homœopathy*, Philadelphia, Boericke & Tafel 1899

Thomas Lindsley Bradford, *The logic of figures or comparative results of homœopathic and other treatments*, Philadelphia, Boericke & Tafel, 1900

Thomas Lindsley Bradford, *Index to homœopathic provings,* Philadelphia, Boericke & Tafel, 1901

Anthony Campbell, *The two faces of homœopathy,* London, Jill Norman & Hale, 1984

Erastus Case, <u>Bureau of Materia Medica</u>, *Transactions of International Hahnemannian Association*, 1915 page 175

N M Choudhuri, *A study on materia medica and repertory*, Calcutta 1916

John Henry Clarke, *Dictionary of homœopathic materia medica*; London, Homœopathic Publishing Co, 3 volumes, 1900 & 1925

John Henry Clarke, <u>*Odium medicum*</u> *and homœopathy:* <u>*The Times*</u> *correspondence*, Homœopathic Publishing Company, London 1888

John Henry Clarke, *Radium as an internal medicine*, London, Homœopathic publishing Co, 1908

Paul François Curie, *Domestic homœopathy*, London, Thomas Hurst, London 1839

Samuel Hahnemann, *The homœopathic medical doctrine or organon of the healing art*, translated by Charles H Devrient from the 4th German edition of 1829, with notes by Samuel Stratten; Dublin, W F Wakeman, 1833

Louis Hyman, *The Jews of Ireland from the earliest times to the year 1910*, London, Jewish Historical Society of England, 1972

Joseph Kidd, On the fever and dysentery of Ireland in 1847, *British Journal of Homœopathy*, pages 85-109, Volume 6, January 1848

Joseph Kidd, Homœopathy in acute diseases; narrative of a mission to Ireland during the famine and pestilence of 1847, pages 202-251 in: Marmaduke B Sampson, *Truths and their reception considered in relation to the doctrine of homœopathy*, London, Samuel Highley, for the British Homœopathic Association, 1849

Joseph Kidd, *The laws of therapeutics*, London, C Kegan Paul, 1881

Joseph Kidd, The last illness of Lord Beaconsfield, *Nineteenth Century,* July 1889

Joseph Kidd, Obituary, *The Lancet.* 21 September 1918

Joseph Kidd, Obituary, *The Times*, 24 August 1918

Walter Kidd, *Joseph Kidd 1824-1918, Limerick London Blackheath; a memoir*, privately printed, 1920, revised 1983

William Flavelle Monypenny & George Earle Buckle, *The life of Benjamin Disraeli, Earl of Beaconsfield*, London, John Murray, 1929

Benoît Mure, *Materia medica or provings of the principal animal and vegetable poisons of the Brazilian Empire and their application in the treatment of disease*, Translated by Charles J Hempel, New York, William Radde; London, James Epps; & Manchester, Henry Turner, 1854

Benoît Mure & Sophie Liet, *L'Homéopathie pure,* Paris, J B Ballière et fils, 1883

Herbert A Roberts *Sensations as if: a repertory of subjective symptoms,* Philadelphia, Boericke & Tafel, 1937

Cecil Woodham Smith, *The great hunger; Ireland 1845-1849*, London, Hamish Hamilton 1962, Penguin 1991

James Ward, *Unabridged dictionary of the sensations as if*, San Francisco, Wobbers Inc., 1939

David Kent Warkentin, *MacRepertory*™ and *ReferenceWorks*™, Kent Homeopathic Associates, California, 1995

Roger van Zandvoort, *Complete repertory*, IRHIS, Leidschendam, 1995

The Samuel Press is named for
Samuel Hahnemann
Rachel Mary Samuel Montagu
and Francis Samuel Treuherz